Active Hope for Your Loved One Who Struggles with Addiction

A Practical Guide to Assist Your Loved One

Bruce A. Lynch

Active Hope for Your Loved One Who Struggles with Addiction

Bruce A. Lynch, MA, LPCS, LPC, LACS, LAC, AADC

Active Hope for Your Loved One Who Struggles with Addiction
by Bruce A. Lynch
Published by Active Hope Counseling,
4466 Holmestown Road, Myrtle Beach, SC 29588
www.ActiveHopeCounseling.com
© 2020

activehopecounseling@gmail.com
Cover by Bruce A. Lynch.
Book ISBN: 978-1-7349084-1-1

I especially wish to dedicate this book and the remainder of my days to my Beautiful and Lovely Twin Daughters, Arianna & Sophia, who have expanded my definition and capacity for love in a manner that was once unimaginable.

Papa Loves You Both Dearly.

Acknowledgements

I want to take a moment to thank all of the individuals that have shown up on my life path to educate, guide, love, and provide sustenance to allow me to overcome the obstacles and challenges that my own life has presented at times. I have learned and acquired much of what I know today simply due to the kindness, generosity, and wisdom of others. I am thankful that what I have learned allows me to live with serenity and peace most days.

As a token of my appreciation and an attempt to pay it forward, I will donate 10% of the net proceeds from this book in any format to two outstanding local non-profits in Horry County, South Carolina.

The first one is the Center for Counseling and Wellness (www.thecenter4counseling.com) which I have had the pleasure to practice at since 2014 assisting individuals, couples, and families. Ron & Roberta Bogle founded the Center to serve anyone and everyone, regardless of the ability to pay, based upon a solid foundation to be the love and light that Jesus demonstrated for us to serve God's Children.

The second non-profit is the North Strand Housing Shelter (www.northstrandhousing-shelter.org) founded by Michael Bolick & Dana Black. Their Mission Statement is "To train and equip leaders... in assisting the underserved (e.g. homeless, hungry, and needy) in the most appropriate way. To find, secure, and provide facilities to house the homeless. To educate those who lack the necessary knowledge to be productive citizens in society using all means available, to include spiritual awareness. To build character, integrity, and sound spiritual values..."

Special Acknowledgement

I would like to recognize Nick Caya and his team at Word-2-Kindle.com (nick@word-2-kindle.com). I am simply amazed at their awesome customer service, excellent suggestions, and guided assistance through each stage of preparing this book for publication. I would highly recommend Word-2-Kindle.com to any aspiring Author(s). Thank you and your team again Nick!

Table of Contents

Table of Contents

Preface

I have had the pleasure and purpose to assist many families who are struggling with addictions. Notice that I stated families, not individuals. Addiction is a family disease, and until it is confronted and accepted as such, little can be done in the way of healing. What if the addicted individual never recovers or dies because of their use of drugs or alcohol or one of the secondary diseases associated with addiction? What then you may ask? Well, to be blunt, that is why I am writing this book.

The idea of this book began in the wake of numerous celebrity tragedies where presumably prescription pill addiction, heroin, and alcohol had claimed its latest victims. As I contemplated writing a book, I recalled the 2012 Grammy's Awards that was held in honor of Whitney Houston. Ms. Houston was an icon, an international figure with a dynamic voice and stage presence that was only rivaled by her inability to refrain from mind-altering, detrimental, addictive substances. In our Reality TV culture, she was captured and sensationalized by the media. Her addiction, subsequent erratic behaviors, and speech have unfortunately been immortalized and ridiculed by comedians and commentaries alike.

Though these tragedies are not an unusual occurrence in everyday America or your local hospital emergency room, they do bring attention, each for a relatively brief time period, to our current culture and lifestyles that allows this to happen. It feels at times that we have accepted that this is the way things are in our society. There have been movements to stop and banish the sale of alcohol and other addictive substances. Addictive substances have been criminalized to deter their use, but in our capitalistic economy, demand automatically equals a supply, despite the tragic costs.

I want to take you, who are presumably a loving family member or friend of someone who is "wasting away" or "spiraling out of control", on a journey of healing and education. I want to enlist your help and provide some basic tools for you to navigate the unpredictable waters of those trapped in the disease of addiction. Laypersons and professionals alike deal with these issues in various ways and prescribe or recommend numerous protocols or suggestions to help and assist with the one you love who is struggling with an addiction. I will challenge you to not "love them to death."

My words will sometimes come from those who I have watched, sometimes gracefully and sometimes tragically, go to "the ends of the earth" trying to find the secret formula to assist their loved one who is struggling with addiction. I heard that Whitney Houston was quoted saying, "I was either my own best friend or my own worst enemy." How true and succinct a statement.

I plan to divide this guidebook up into various chapters to deal with the host of issues that are associated with this grossly misunderstood or mismanaged subject. My sincere desire is to provide you with immediate and effective principles for dealing with the one in your life who is struggling with addiction. But first I have one question to ask... Whose behavior can you control?

Chapter 1
Whose Behavior Can You Control?

William Glasser, MD, the father of Reality Therapy and Choice Theory began some of his counseling sessions with the question which is the title of this chapter. There is only one completely right answer. Have you determined it yet? Yes, say it aloud- "My own." Well done, now repeat this declarative statement one hundred times a day. Serenity will be restored almost immediately once you fully accept its implications.

In speaking with parents and family members who are employing rational thought processing, they always seemed amazed at their loved ones' completely irrational behavior and actions, despite the apparent negative consequences of their continued use of drugs and alcohol. Loss of jobs, jail, prison, ill health and diseases, loss of opportunity, financial ruin, loss of children, divorce, or anything else seemingly of value or purposeful meaning are cast aside for one more high, one more drinking binge, one more fix, one more...?

Attempting to understand your loved one's illogical reasoning is where you need to make the first correction in your thinking. It is important to adjust to the reality of the addicted individual's life. Nothing else matters but "one more (fill in the blank with their favorite addictive substance)".

Let's go back to the caveman days of the early Neanderthal man. Addiction hijacks the "old brain's" reward circuitry. I am going to steer clear of the numerous medical or neuropsychological technical terms and leave that to the medical professionals, but this is an important point to provide some understanding of why your loved one cannot "stay stopped." Mark Twain, classic American author and humorist once stated, "Quitting smoking is easy; I've done it hundreds of times." Twain's quote, and current brain research, both have highlighted the fact that Addiction not only hijacks the oldest part of the brain, but addiction also moves to the forefront in terms of motivating and dominating behavior.

All of us have an innate drive to breathe, eat food, drink water, procreate (have sex), and sleep. The brain's internal motivational drive and corresponding cerebral cortex (the thinking and planning part of the brain) collaborate with each other to satisfy these innate drives for survival. Unfortunately, when a person becomes addicted, the addiction itself is now the main driving force. Folks who struggle with addictions give up the other drives and may go without food, water, sex, and sleep, for extended time periods. Yet, they will always strive to satisfy their addiction by any means necessary.

This is where you come in. Has your loved one lied to you to get money or free time to satisfy his or her Addiction? Have they made promises they have been unable to keep? Have they sung the Alcoholic or Addict "National Anthem" of "I'll never do that again", only to repeat an even greater fiasco or harm in the future? Yep, it sounds like the "old brain" has been hijacked.

We are no longer dealing with the "apple of your eye" as your son or daughter appeared when they were born, or that handsome and promising man you married, or that trusting and caring beautiful woman who gave you her hand in marriage. If you can accept this point, my friend, we have a good chance of working in a productive direction together. If you still need convincing, the Addiction will do this for us in time, but you have been warned.

My intent is not to dehumanize or condemn the loved one in your life. I am going to ask that you take a step back physically, and mentally, from the situation you are currently in to look at what is really happening. I am quite sure you never considered that Addiction would become a major factor in your life. It just happened.

4

However, by taking a literal and figurative step back from the process, you will be able to gain a greater perspective on what has been occurring all along.

Denial is the first culprit we need to address. Think of the number of internal excuses you have made for your loved one such as: He/She has had a hard life; He/She works hard; His/Her (i.e., mother, father, sibling, friend) died when they were young; He/She has an incurable disease, amputated limb, etc.... Now think of the lies you have told to cover up their misbehaviors such as: calling into their work or school when they had a hangover or long night; lies to the doctor or physician; lies to Teachers or Coaches; lies to those at your church or workplace.

I intentionally use the strong term "lie" to exemplify how you have had to alter your moral compass in the face of their addiction. But what would my (i.e. Boss, Parents, Friends, Church, Neighbors) think? Let that worry go, as this is your life and your business. Everyone has skeletons in the closet, and the picture-perfect families may just have larger closets. This book is not for anyone but you.

A little word of advice is to not disclose to your loved one who is struggling with addiction, that you are reading this book. They will attempt to sabotage some of the wisdom contained in this volume to counteract your efforts. In addition, heightening their suspicion that you are aware of their schemes will simply force them to develop new schemes. Quantum physics has shown that simply observing something, anything, by itself, alters it. Keep this wisdom to yourself and/or another concerned individual and simply attempt to enact some of the principles contained in this book.

You will not get 100% effective results 100% of the time. I do not wish to make any claims that this is a miracle solution in written form. However, I do believe that you will get healthier and become better equipped in dealing with and responding to your loved one's incessant demands if you apply the principles in this book. Notice that I did not say react because that has been the problem up until now. You have simply been reacting to life and your loved one in a haphazard manner without any plan of action.

Think about it, as I guess that you have had several successes in your life up until this point to draw from. In your past successes in life, either in work, school, or family and marital relations, I imagine you have had a plan or script from which you worked, to achieve your goals. For example, to graduate from any level of education, one must take time to study, pass exams, and apply for higher levels of education. In order to be successful, you must gather new information and then apply that information to make new decisions.

Another goal for this book is to give you new or more practical information to help your loved one. I am sure that your intentions for helping are pure. Unfortunately, we are not judged by our intentions, rather, only by our actions.

I will start by attempting to relieve you of any guilt that you have been carrying as to how some of your past actions (or lack of actions) have created the current situation with your loved one and his/her addiction. Guess what? YOU did not CREATE their addiction. You cannot CONTROL their addiction. You cannot CURE their addiction.

All parents will carry some inherent guilt that they should have done this or should not have done that when little Johnny and sweet Suzy were small, to keep their child from becoming addicted. Not true! You are not God and you do not control the Universe.

I want to relieve you of this guilt. I also want to heighten your level of awareness surrounding your own guilt, as this is probably the main source of motivation your loved one is using to manipulate you. Those who are connected to our heartstrings can hurt us and manipulate us the most. We cannot help but think the best of our loved ones, and knowing that we may have failed them at some time in the past drives us to want to make up for that lack in the present. Unfortunately, it is like wearing a big banner that says, "I am easily duped or conned; please ask me for money (to pay your rent, for gas, for food, etc...)". The past is the past.

Chapter 1

By reading this book, you are demonstrating that you are a concerned individual who is trying to arm yourself with the facts. You are taking active steps to assist your loved one who is struggling with addiction and are demonstrating that you desperately wish to save them, as you have witnessed them dying by the fading light of substance abuse.

Chapter 2
Are You a Victim or a Volunteer?

Some parents and loved ones complain that their child is constantly lying, stealing, or even threatening them. This does not have to be the case. I am not able to tell you personally when enough is enough without knowing the particulars of your situation. However, I would say if verbal or physical threats have been made, it is time to allow the addicted individual to fend for themselves in another living situation outside of your home if they happen to still be residing with you.

Look up on the internet the statistics on domestic violence and you will find a near-perfect correlation between violent assaults and alcohol/drug use. Due to the seriousness of this problem, there are professionals and courts in your area that can assist you. Remember, your safety comes first. If anything happens to you, who will take care of the one you are trying to help? Please visit my website for more details on how to consult attorneys or court representatives that can assist you via the criminal justice system with your loved one (www.active hopecounseling.com).

Along these lines, I have assisted parents who had paid out of pocket for their son's or daughter's 7th, 8th..., or 15th... rehab treatment episode. Even with moderate treatment expenditures or costs for state treatment facilities, these numbers would add up quickly.

Parents are paying for rehabilitation services for children who were well into adulthood (chronologically speaking). I will give some recommendations for these situations later. Just know that there are some remarkably effective programs that are free or cost extraordinarily little in regard to fees because the participant helps to pay their way through WORK.

Work? What a concept some of you may ask. If you have been providing for the addicted individual's basic needs (food, water, shelter, and possibly transportation, school, clothes, medical bills), I ask you, why would your loved one have to work? When the proverbial "poop" hits the fan, you may have financed their stay in a 30-day rehab dedicated to helping them find their inner selves through holistic care including: massages, yoga, Tai Chi, gourmet organic nutritional options, and spectacular vistas over- looking nature's wonder and splendor. Are you now beginning to see how you may have been unintentionally prolonging their walk in their addiction by coming to their rescue?

I am not saying that you have done a single thing wrong, but you would not be reading this book had your methods been effective. All I am suggesting is that you be willing to try a different approach. I am intentionally being slow about offering specific advice because I do understand that you have truly been doing what you have thought was best. Again, I ask though, how have your methods worked so far? Insanity is defined in the twelve-step programs by "doing the same thing over and over while expecting a different result." Are you guilty of repeating the same patterns regarding your loved one?

Are you ready to do what is best for your loved one, not what simply aids or boosts your ego or feelings? At times, I know my words may sound blunt or harsh, but I am concerned with actually helping you make positive changes. Feelings are not facts. Positive results will be the reward for enacting some of the principles contained in this book. Are you prepared to allow your loved one to be homeless or incarcerated, versus the option of "enabling them to death?"

One of the first family groups I had the pleasure of facilitating had a mother in her sixties who came to meetings only to help other parents who were struggling with their loved one's addiction issues. She always would share the statement above about enabling your loved one to death, and I could see the impact it would have on the other parents in the room. She had dealt with her son and his addiction for over thirty years. He was now in his mid-forties and still relapsing after brief periods of sobriety. She had made a vow to herself that she would not contribute to his death in any way by funding or providing any resources that would enable him in his addiction. She had helped him numerous times when he was embracing recovery, but the moment he lapsed or started showing signs of using again, she would withdraw support and allow him to experience the consequences of his own behavior.

Some may ask, why did he keep relapsing, and how is what she did considered correct if he continued to relapse? Well, this will have to be answered in a two-part discussion. The mother did the right thing for herself, regardless of whether it was right for him. I will argue that this was the best tactic she could have enlisted, as her son evidenced a chronic use and addictive lifestyle for so many years that any further enabling of his addiction could have pushed him over the edge to his own death. Morally and psychologically, the mother made a sound decision. She was the one that was going to have to live with her contributions should he have died due to one of her enabling attempts.

I cannot tell you when or how to enact your version of tough love, as this will be as unique as your own family situation. I have assisted families who inadvertently neglected other siblings and loved ones in their attempts to help the "problem-child" of the family. Remember to consider all members of the family when deciding how and when to set boundaries.

Chapter 3
Let's Try Something Different

Please do not be offended, but if your methods were 100% successful, you would not be reading this book. I am sure that you are an intelligent, compassionate, and caring soul. However, you need to recognize that there is already a habitual pattern in place between the way you and your loved one are reacting and responding to each other's actions and deeds. Think about all of the automatic or habitual mini conversations you have every day with your loved ones, co-workers, cashiers at your favorite shopping locations, etc.... Aren't most of these conversations similar, no matter the day or time?

Much of what we communicate is done habitually, especially with people close to us, which in turn makes us feel comfortable, intimate, and safe in most situations. However, if you have been battling a loved one's addiction, these habitual conversations have probably garnered a severely negative tone by the time you decided to read this book. It is what it is, but it does not have to stay that way.

Think before you speak (I know, what a concept), but seriously think. I want you to simply ask yourself before you speak or lash out at your loved one: "Are the words that are going to come out of my mouth going to bring us closer together or move us further apart?" Nagging or complaining serves no beneficial purpose, period. Acceptance and tolerance will gain you temporary favor, and assertive communication will help you stand your ground, without compromising the relationship. Remember, you cannot help someone who is emotionally or mentally distant from you. I am not suggesting that you accept unacceptable behavior, but I do recommend that you attempt to understand what your addicted loved one is experiencing. Remarks such as "It must be really tough (or painful) to deal with all (list all of the consequences) that you have to deal with," or "I feel sad watching you struggle with this awful disease," externalizes the problem. Externalizing the problem can remove the morality and character assassination component that is a problem for most addicts. You cannot shame or guilt addicts more than they can do to themselves. Actually, this personal guilt and shame is a key element in the addiction cycle. Becoming "comfortably numb" and seeking oblivion are the goals of most substance abusers who are in the middle or late stages of their addiction.

Tolerance, love, and understanding in tandem with a willingness and patience to assist if the loved one wishes to seek help, will be your most effective tool. Physically and psychologically removing yourself from the harmful actions and effects of your loved one with an addiction problem will begin to allow you to gain important attributes that will serve all parties better than other, harsher methods. You need to always remember that there is nothing that you can or cannot do to make your loved one continue to use or choose to stop using. This is the key to keeping your sanity. Knowing you are consistent and supportive will be one of the most important legacies you can imprint on your loved one's heart and mind.

Chapter 4
This is a Deadly Disease.

As I write this, I am recounting the cherished souls of the individuals who have succumbed to this affliction. I cannot help but wonder what else, if anything, could have been done to prevent the tragedy of the loss of life due to drug addiction and alcoholism? In my professional pursuits as a Therapist and my own participation in recovery groups, I must admit that I am somewhat desensitized to the loss of life as a direct result of substance use. I am not proud to say this, and it troubles me that my desensitization to the loss of human life is a direct consequence of these individuals' choices and actions.

Yet, I have also seen countless others restore their lives from a state of incomprehensible demoralization to sober, active, and vibrant recovery-oriented lives. I have seen people in recovery filled with purpose and passion and acts of service and expressions of gratitude. I continue to ponder as to why some individuals are able to recover while others are not.

There is not an easy explanation as to why certain individuals are successful in their recovery attempts while others are not, or else it would have been discussed or written about previously. I believe it is necessary to treat and counsel individuals in a uniquely personal and holistic manner. Many issues stem from one's childhood and family of origin. These issues are not readily "fixable" and may have been suppressed for many years. They may have been the source of the aggravation of mental health disorders that have persisted below the level of consciousness for many years. As expected, early intervention after a child or adult experiences any sort of trauma is key to prevent issues in the future.

However, many times families or caregivers do not seek appropriate treatment services available, because of their own personal guilt or shame, or simply out of fear of legal consequences or incrimination. One of the hardest issues to assist an individual with is to help him/her acknowledge some form of abuse, especially sexual abuse, molestation, or incest. It is particularly challenging to attempt to help someone process why his/her caregiver (i.e. Mother, Father, Aunt, Uncle, or Grandparents) did not step up to the rescue and stop further incidents from happening. It is nearly unthinkable to imagine that an adult of any relation, or even a bystander, would allow another adult to prey on a child in any manner.

Having worked at numerous workplaces over my career, I am intimately aware of cases that involve adults not stopping or reporting abuse. Upon completing an intake and evaluation of a 55+ older "Grandmother" who was referred by our Department of Social Services, I consulted with another Therapist who had worked with her on a prior admission to that treatment facility. I was new in the helping profession at the time and will admit that I had possessed profound naivety regarding being able to identify other's motives initially. Fortunately, the other Counselor was there to assist. The grandmother was referred to our Treatment Agency because her live-in boyfriend, who also supplied her crack-cocaine habit, had fondled her granddaughter. The grandmother had custody of her granddaughter because her daughter had special needs, and that daughter had also been sexually molested by one of her mother's previous boyfriend(s). The granddaughter was a result of one of these previous sexual encounters. The Grandmother was there simply to comply with state agency requirements to allow her to keep custody of her granddaughter. Custody of the granddaughter would keep a "substantial" monthly check and other benefits rolling in, which would permit her to keep her drug addiction supported. I hope you can now see clearly how generations of abuse are persisted without appropriate intervention.

Chapter 5
Methadone Clinics & Opioid Treatment Programs

If you have a loved one who is contemplating getting help, and opiates or opioids are their preferred drug of choice, they may be more open to finding assistance through a Methadone Clinic. Methadone clinics are now being recognized as Opioid Treatment Programs in an attempt to break negative stigmas. To give you an introductory overview of how these clinics operate, it is important to distinguish between public agencies and for-profit clinics. For-profit clinics may have a bottom line they need to consider in providing their services, but they are still strictly regulated through state and federal agencies, guidelines, and mandates.

For-profit clinics operate in every major city and town, and there is usually not a shortage of individuals requesting assistance. Some clinics are strict on their intake and evaluation procedures, including not allowing individuals who are continuously abusing other substances to participate or stay in their program. Other clinics will turn a blind eye to patients who are still having difficulty maintaining abstinence from non-opioid substances, including marijuana and cocaine. Most programs, however, have strict policies for patients who are continuously abusing benzodiazepines (i.e. Xanax®, Valium®, Ativan®, etc.) due to their synergistic effect as a central nervous system depressant, along with their daily dose of Methadone.

Please note that Methadone is an Opioid Agonist and will "satisfy" the drug seeker's physiological and psychological craving. This being stated, the patient may appear "high" or impaired on methadone if their dose is higher than needed. Most programs will allow patients to increase their dose, daily or weekly depending on their time in the program, in an attempt to reach a stabilized therapeutic dose. There is a tremendous amount of research supporting this concept and I would concur that a patient should be allowed to reach a stabilized therapeutic dosage. Reaching a stabilized therapeutic dose will allow the patient to turn his/her attention to addressing recovery and other life issues, such as vocational, educational, family, and other holistically restorative activities.

Please understand that there exists the possibility for patients to "abuse" the system and request doses that may be higher than needed. Most programs have a maximum dose that a patient may receive without incurring further metabolic blood tests (peak and trough levels) to determine the exact level of methadone in their bloodstream. This is supported by the fact that health and medical conditions can and do affect the breakdown of methadone in the bloodstream, and that at times, higher than originally recommended doses may be recommended.

Please note that pain clinics and physicians also utilize methadone for assisting with the alleviation of pain symptoms. Actually, most of the tragic news one may hear about someone overdosing or dying from methadone does not originate from a Methadone Clinic or Opioid Treatment Program. Rather, these deaths and overdoses occur as a result of an illicit transfer of prescribed medications from physicians in pill form. Methadone Clinics routinely use a liquid form or dose of methadone, rather than pills. Patients typically must show up daily to the clinic to receive their daily dose, as this ensures compliance with the program standards, and maintains safety for the public at large.

It is only after a patient meets various criteria, typically including being abstinent from other illicit substances, that he/she is allowed to receive take-home doses of methadone in an earned-privilege manner. The fact that patients do have to show up daily and receive their dose, may actually benefit them from a behavioral therapy perspective. Daily practices help the patient place a focus and priority on recovery, and establish a healthier routine, than what their potential income and illicit drug-seeking behaviors may have included. I believe this point may be the most important for a loved one or family member to understand and accept, to assist with their reluctance about allowing or suggesting that their loved one attend a Methadone Clinic.

Drug addiction affects men and women in different ways. Males are more likely to commit a crime to obtain money to purchase their drugs of choice. Women tend to have the ability to participate in sex-oriented industries for money or drugs to support their habits. Please keep this in mind if your reluctance or opposition is still present. Consider methadone as a much healthier alternative to jail, a criminal record, sexually transmitted infections, and the litany of unmentionables that are alive and present in the underbelly of the heroin and opioid epidemic crisis.

Methadone Clinics typically have a physician, who is Licensed and Board-Certified in

Addiction Medicine, and State Certified or Licensed Addiction Counselors, who provide limited Individual Counseling (due to their Caseload). Methadone clinics also provide recovery and treatment groups to their patients who wish to learn new information and resources that could be of assistance in their recovery and in maintaining their adherence to their new lifestyle. Of course, the quality and quantity of counseling vary greatly from each clinic or program. Availability and quality of counseling may be helpful questions to ask the intake person should you wish to call and inquire about services on behalf of your loved one.

So, is a methadone clinic the right option for your Loved One? Well, the litmus test may be whether other attempts on your loved one's behalf have ended up being an exercise in futility. If so, then please consider a methadone clinic as an option. I have witnessed the lives of individuals and families changed when participating in these programs, seriously. Yet, I am also aware of how certain programs could improve their focus and treatment protocols to assist the individual patient in a more helpful manner. All in all, these programs need to be a viable option for you or your family member to consider if other methods have not been successful.

Chapter 6
Suboxone® & Zubsolv®
(Buprenorphine and Naloxone)

Many Methadone Clinics also prescribe Suboxone® or generic alternatives. I am a big fan of these alternatives to methadone as they are partial opioid agonists. Simply stated, Suboxone® satisfies the craving yet does not fully activate the opioid receptor so the "high" that may be experienced by the use of methadone is nullified.

The upside to this alternative to methadone, regarding the treatment of Opioid Use Disorders, is the discretion and privacy in the setting that one may receive treatment at, if they choose. They can seek out a Physician who prescribes these medications out of their private practice. Physicians who choose to prescribe these medications attend specialized training. They are strictly regulated by DEA guidelines in the number of patients they may serve and in the review of their medical files for adherence to suggested protocols for delivering treatment. As a plus, the stigmas still associated with other options, such as attending methadone clinics or treatment programs, are not present when working directly with a physician out of their private practice. The individual simply attends a medical appointment at a physician's office. Many folks report that they prefer this level of privacy and confidentiality.

Remember that we are dealing with an epidemic that does not discriminate when we are speaking of individuals who are caught in the grips of opioid addiction. Many individuals are reluctant to seek treatment because they feel that their job or standing in the community may be affected if others find out that they are suffering from a substance use disorder. This simple fact has probably led to more unnecessary tragic outcomes and prevented or prolonged one's desire to seek and actually receive the treatment they need.

Typically, physicians who prescribe Suboxone® or Zubsolv® require that their patients attend counseling and/or participate in 12-Step recovery support groups to bolster their recovery efforts. Some physicians even have Certified or Licensed Addiction Counselors available as part of their practice to assist with this requirement. The good news is that more physicians are choosing to prescribe these medications, which means more physicians are becoming acutely aware and knowledgeable on how to recognize and assist with addiction issues. These efforts have been aided by a recent Surgeon's General Letter to Physicians (*visit my website for a web link to this letter) to screen for, and provide safeguards to assist, patients who may be vulnerable to becoming addicted to prescription painkillers.

Chapter 7

Your Options to Find and Finance Treatment ... Free, Sell an Organ, Coercion, or Speak to a Judge

If you have succeeded in your efforts to convince your loved one to get help, or if he/she has experienced a twisted and sordid series of events that have opened his/her eyes for the need for a new way of life, you may be asking, what now? With an overwhelming abundance of treatment options, you or your loved one may not know where to begin. I hope that you find some direction and solace by the end of this chapter and that you have a better sense of what is available regarding professional services for you and your family.

The good news is that if you have health insurance, your options are increased. Private health insurers (i.e. Blue Cross Blue Shield, Humana, United, Aetna, Cigna, Tricare) may need a pre-approval before deciding to cover a residential treatment program, but they will evaluate the need on a case by case scenario.

The private carrier will need to speak to the person who is covered and is requesting services to accurately assess the appropriate level of treatment coverage. Please expect the health insurance company to initially recommend a lower level of services, such as Individual Counseling or an Intensive-Outpatient Program (IOP), as this is a less expensive option for the insurer.

As a tip, I will recommend first selecting several inpatient programs if the need necessitates this (more on this later), and the treatment program will do its utmost to make sure your loved one gets coverage. This ensures that the program will get paid (welcome to managed health care services). If you contact the treatment program that you are interested in, that program will go above and beyond (hopefully) to make sure your loved one successfully navigates the hurdles necessary to utilize the benefits of their health coverage.

In selecting a treatment program for private health insured individuals, one could call the insurance company to see what programs in your area are covered under your plan, prior to contacting random treatment centers or programs. Of course, you could call the treatment program, and then inquire about their credentials for different health insurance plans or companies.

Expect that the insurer may only cover a portion of the treatment program's recommended stay. For example, if the treatment program recommends 28 days of residential treatment, the insurer may only opt to pay for 14 or 21 days of this time. Most treatment programs will work with you and expedite services or adjust the discharge plan to accommodate this modification for your loved one. My general rule of thumb states that (*almost) any treatment is better than no treatment

In selecting a program, you may consult reviews online, and/or call the programs you are interested in. Be sure to ask them about their services and how much actual treatment time (individual therapy, group therapy, recreational therapy, medication-assisted treatment options, co-occurring treatment options) your loved one will receive each day. Most private treatment programs are a "medical model treatment program," which means that there will be a physician (MD or DO) or psychiatrist (preferably one who specializes in addictions) on staff that will be able to treat other mental health disorders that may accompany the addiction issues.

Mental health symptoms or disorders such as Depression, Anxiety, Bipolar Disorder, and ADHD should be addressed. Treating these underlying mental health issues is an important component of treatment, as many medical professionals speculate that substance use is at times a way to self-medicate or regulate other symptoms of other treatable disorders.

If your loved one has Medicaid or Medicare, there are still many options, however, certain private treatment programs may not accept these types of insurance. Again, as a starting point, you could call the managed health care provider number which is listed on the back of the health insurance card and inquire about which programs may be covered under their plan. Even though this option is perhaps a little more limited, there are still vibrant and wonderful programs that will be able to assist your loved one through this pivotal transitional stage, as your loved one begins to search for a new way of life free from the influence of alcohol or drugs.

If your loved one is a mother, she and the children may be eligible for various family programs. These programs are growing in popularity because of current amounts of ample state and federal funding. The research clearly demonstrates that children greatly benefit from therapeutic services and a stable environment, especially if they experienced the chaos of living with a mother who is dependent on mood-altering substances. Some mothers themselves have been victims of domestic violence and other forms of abuse. If the children were present on some of these occasions, one can easily garner the appropriateness of these types of family residential programs. Typically, these programs only accept children in their pre-teens or younger and have a maximum number of children that they will allow to stay with the mother (i.e. two or three children).

Regardless of your insurance status, other residential programs that are faith-based or 12-Step oriented may be of great benefit to you or your loved one. While Christian faith-based programs may not be suitable for everyone depending upon their beliefs, convictions, or other worldviews, they are available. Many folks will tout these programs as the beginnings of their new way of life, free from the self-imprisonment of their dependence on their drug(s) of preference. You can research online available programs in your local community or state or speak to local churches and pastors for their suggestions.

Please note that many of these programs do not have licensed or certified staff members. Many faith-based programs will recruit former successful participants of the program to facilitate additional services to new attendees. Also, most of these programs ARE NOT A MEDICAL MODEL program; therefore, they typically do not have a physician or psychiatrist on staff. They also may not allow participants to take medications for psychological conditions. Please check on the restrictions of theses programs prior to delivering your loved one to their front door.

I am keen on 12-step residential programs as a viable alternative for many seeking help from alcohol and drug addiction. Many of these programs REQUIRE that participants WORK to pay for their stay. The participant is either given a job at the facility, or he/she is allowed to work off-site, typically in locations where the residential program has an ongoing relationship with the nearby employers. These programs require participants to attend 12-step meetings (AA or NA) and to obtain a sponsor or mentor. Participants must remain actively engaged in "working the steps," referring to the twelve steps covered in a later chapter in more detail.

Both faith-based and 12-Step recovery residential programs may be viable options worthy of consideration, after you assess the particulars of your loved one's situation. Some require the participants to be able-bodied and may not be able to assist folks with certain disabilities. These programs may not be suitable for everyone, but if lack of finances or lack of appropriate insurance coverage exists, please consider faith-based or 12-step based residential programs.

One benefit of these programs includes having a tight-knit group of peers who are in similar stages of recovery and can identify with the struggles that your loved one is experiencing. I encourage you to recognize the importance of this dynamic principle.

Your loved one has endured years of trials & tribulations with folks looking at them with a mixture of pity and disgust. The guilt and shame associated with addiction is truly immeasurable. There is a dynamic and radically transformative power of being accepted by a loving group of recovering peers. These peers not only understand the pains and errors of their past but accept other addicts or alcoholics (these terms are said in a respectful and non-stigmatizing manner within the rooms of 12-step programs) all the more for having been through similar hard times. The recovery peers want nothing more than for all members of the group to stay sober one day at a time and carry the message of recovery to the next sufferer.

Admittedly, this concept may be challenging for some who are not familiar with 12-step programs or other recovery services. I could only illustrate the point by comparing the camaraderie that our active military and veterans speak of when they have been through Hell on Earth and lived to share about it. (Thank you to all who have served & fought in the Armed Forces to preserve our Right to Freedom and Free Speech).

The value of work is well demonstrated from a biblical, functional, and evolutionary perspective. When an addict engages in one of these treatment programs, he/she can earn a sense of respect and dignity that they may not have had prior to treatment. Achieving this simple quality alone is priceless, regardless of the re-medial tasks that are often part of the program. Also, the principle of "move a muscle, change a thought" becomes an active agent of change. In certain instances, one could make the argument that these type of programs that require addicts to actively work as part of their recovery stay are more beneficial than simply sending the addict to a rehab facility to enjoy spa-like amenities.

The point I am trying to make is that the path-way to recovery is large and wide. I encourage both professionals and laypersons to be more receptive to the options that one may have to begin his/her journey in recovery. I would not ever tell a person that a treatment program is not a good option, unless there have been seri-ous viable complaints or violations on their re-cord (and these do exist, far and few between).

We are moving toward what has profession-ally been referred to as a recovery-oriented ser-vices paradigm. This paradigm is one that tends to be inclusive, rather than exclusive, regarding pathways to recovery. Additional information about this topic is presented later in this book.

There may be a need to visit the emergency room at your nearest hospital if you are not able to locate the appropriate services for your loved one in a timely manner. Please note there are only two substances that are currently being abused that could cause death or other near-fatal consequences from withdrawal and those are Alcohol and Benzodiazepines (i.e. Xanax®, Valium®, Klonopin®, Ativan®). Barbiturates are much more rarely prescribed today because of their relatively low lethal dose but can also be deadly if one should withdrawal suddenly without the appropriate medical protocols.

Preferably, you or your loved one will be able to locate an appropriate medical detoxification facility that will allow your loved one to safely taper or withdrawal from any of these physiologically dependent substances. In order to safely detox from abused substances, your loved one should have their vitals monitored under the care of a qualified physician.

Many inpatient programs will have your loved one in a detoxification unit when they first enter the program. During this time, various things are closely observed, including the patient's pulse, blood pressure, and any other medical issues that may have been noted upon admission. While it is arguably stated that only benzodiazepines and alcohol necessitate the need for medically monitored detoxification services, these programs can also offer assistance and other compassionate medical services to those in withdrawal from other narcotics and heroin. The withdrawal from opiates is not life-threatening in most circumstances unless they exacerbate other medical issues. However, withdrawal is quite unpleasant and upsetting.

Detoxification programs can offer various medical protocols to make withdrawal a more humane process for your loved one. Remember, if you are unable to locate a treatment program to assist your loved one, please do not hesitate to take him/her to the nearest hospital emergency room.

Please note that during withdrawal, your loved one may express self-harming or suicidal thoughts or ideation. These statements should be taken seriously. I encourage you to consult with a mental health professional, or simply call 911 to have the paramedics and local law enforcement personnel assist in ensuring the safety of your loved one.

If your loved one has been arrested, is currently in jail, or has a pending court date, I would strongly advise you to consult with the court or a legal representative about options for treatment in lieu of simply serving a traditional jail or prison sentence. Due to an increase in funding on both the state and local level, many more options are now currently available to offenders than have ever been available before. Whether this is a first or thirtieth charge, the courts, and most judges, would prefer to sentence an addict to a treatment program, rather than simply imprisonment.

Pre-trial intervention services, and other similar programs, offer individuals who have committed a crime the option of completing counseling and other group services. These services typically include a drug awareness and educational component, plus testimonies from others who were in similar circumstances and have recovered their life. Pre-trial intervention programs typically have mandatory requirements such as getting a job, being subjected to frequent urinary drug screens, and simply being monitored by court liaisons. Court liaisons typically are well versed in encouraging participants with a gentle mixture of the old metaphor of the "stick (jail time) and carrot (charges dismissed-absence of jail time)."

If felony charges are involved, please inquire about "Drug Court" programs that may be available. These programs have strict and arduous guidelines and requirements but allow a participant to remain free from incarceration, so the individual can work. For someone accused of a felony to participate in a drug court program, he/she must engage recovery through the attendance of various nightly treatment groups. Other strict program guidelines include having a job and testing negative on drug screens. Due to the increased demands of these programs, not all participants successfully complete them. Failure to complete the drug court program will likely result in the original stiff punishment or lengthy prison sentence being enforced. For individuals who are fortunate enough to complete these programs, they will prove to court officials, and themselves, that they do have what it takes to lead a life free of the influence of mood-altering substances. These individuals will also be free from the associated criminal behavior that typically accompanies drug-seeking behaviors that funds their addiction.

You and/or your loved one may wish to meet with a Licensed Therapist (i.e. Licensed Professional Counselor, Licensed Master's Social Worker, Licensed Marriage & Family Therapist) to help through the recovery process. Preferably, the therapist would be credentialed by a state or national certification or licensure board, regarding working with people with substance use disorders (i.e. Certified Addictions Counselor or Licensed Addiction Counselor). If your loved one is open to going to a residential treatment program, establishing this relationship with a Licensed Therapist will greatly enhance his/her recovery maintenance portfolio once they are released from their treatment program. A Licensed Therapist is skilled in enhancing a client 's internal motivation and can help bolster his/her decision-making skills. A Licensed Therapist will also have increased knowledge of recovery resources in your area, and also should have appropriate recommendations on how to tap into the local recovery community.

Chapter 8

So, What's Up with the 12 Steps and Groups such as AA and NA... Pros & Cons

First and foremost, I am not speaking on behalf or as a representative of any associated recovery groups. However, I will attempt to give a brief summary of these programs, to increase your understanding of how they work. I will also share my own personal understanding and knowledge of 12-step programs. I believe these programs are vitally important to the recovery movement. I hope to offer an objective, yet realistic, perspective to better increase your understanding to help your loved one navigate the roads of recovery.

The first 12-step program I would like to discuss is Alcoholics Anonymous (AA). The AA program has been around in its current form since the 1930s. This program was founded by two drunks (self-admittedly) named Bill Wilson and Dr. Bob Smith. These men collaborated to write the Big Book of Alcoholics Anonymous. The "Big Book" contains the original twelve steps, that have been adopted by hundreds of other self-help groups. The popularity of AA groups has expanded greatly, and groups can be found worldwide and even on cruise ship itineraries (seriously). I am confident there are numerous AA groups in your local area.

The first 164 pages of the Big Book of Alcoholics Anonymous contains the basic elements of the twelve-step program for recovery. The Twelve Steps are outlined and explained in varying degrees of specificity, with various suggestions regarding how one may begin to work on these steps in his/her own life.

It is suggested that a person who joins the program obtains sponsorship. A sponsor is a recovering member of the program who has worked through the steps and has maintained continuous sobriety for a certain amount of time. More years of sobriety do not necessarily qualify one person to be a better sponsor than another, but I think the sponsor should have a minimum of one year of sobriety before they help lead others out of the dark. The current recommendation is that women obtain a female sponsor and that men obtain a male sponsor (for heterosexual individuals though other lifestyle preferences are also accommodated).

Alcoholics Anonymous programs offer meetings in churches, clubhouses, and other unique venues such as coffee shops. Given the current COVID-19 crisis, the availability of online 12-step groups has also sharply increased. Daily attendance at these groups is not uncommon, and some individuals find it beneficial to attend multiple meetings per day. Meetings times vary, and some clubhouses in more metropolitan areas have a meeting every hour on the hour throughout the day and night. Given the fact that most private & public treatment programs incorporate and encourage attendance at 12-step groups, I hope you will be able to understand the potential importance of these programs.

I personally have experienced the "miracle" of working the twelve steps in a sequential manner with the assistance of a sponsor (RIP & May God Bless the Spirit of Verne C., my First Sponsor). With firsthand knowledge and hopefully the practice of the principles, I hope to illuminate that the AA program is more than individuals in a room sharing the mess they have made of their lives.

It is important that you or your loved one understand the "singleness of purpose" of the AA program. In Alcoholics Anonymous, members are asked to only share their struggles with alcohol and refrain from discussing other drugs as a part of their story in the meeting places. To simply explain the rationale for this decision, AA programs do not wish to isolate those who have not abused other substances. Many current members of AA have multiple decades of sobriety and would not have any frame of reference for current street drugs of abuse.

Not all 12-step programs require a singleness of purpose. Narcotics Anonymous (NA), which was founded in 1953, also incorporates the twelve steps as part of their program of recovery. An individual may share about their use of drugs and alcohol at an NA meeting without reprimand.

Both AA and NA programs have "open" and "closed" meetings of various formats. Everyone is welcomed to attend "open" meetings. Yet, at "closed" meetings, attendance is limited to those who have substance abuse issues and identify with the following statement: "The only requirement for A.A. membership is a desire to stop drinking." The same rule about closed and open meetings is applicable for the NA program. When attending 12-step group meetings, it is quite common to hear the term Alcoholic or Addict thrown around, without having the same negative stereotypical implications generally associated with these labels. Twelve-step programs claim that everyone has earned their seat in the program and that the term Alcoholic is a step up from a Drunk, as is the term Addict a step up from a Junkie. Of course, it is a personal and individual choice to identify with these labels, and these are not requirements to attend a meeting.

If you are reading this book on behalf of a loved one, you too may benefit from the associated 12-step programs of Al-Anon or Nar-Anon. Both programs incorporate the twelve steps and help YOU identify how you can heal from the destruction that loving someone who has a drinking or drug addiction problem has caused in your life.

The Twelve Steps are a spiritual path for folks to recover. Individuals who have been to hell, and do not want to go back, may find a light at the end of the tunnel through the practice of these steps. The programs are non-denominational, and do not dictate who or what one designates as his/her "Higher Power." Many Fundamentalists may have a concern with the flexibility of choosing a higher power, but I encourage you to not limit your treatment options because of this flexibility. If religion were the sole answer, we would not have alcoholic or addicted clergy who will tout the benefits of these recovery communities. The Twelve Steps are more of a practical pathway, via spiritual principles, to help clear up the wreckage of one's past and connect to others. The Twelve Steps help an individual to be able to assert himself/herself in their community as an example of the redemptive power of Spirit (GOD).

Being a spiritual path, the first step of the twelve steps involves an admission of one's powerlessness over their substance of choice. After this initial admission, an additional series of steps involve accepting the assistance of a Higher Power (GOD) to assist in one's recovery. After accepting the assistance of a higher power, the next steps include a housecleaning and moral inventory. These steps allow individuals to make an honest self-assessment, recognizing attributes and liabilities that they may have to contend with for the duration of their recovery. Additional steps include making amends to individuals they have harmed which allows a person to feel comfortable in his/her environment and community and banishes the fear of running into others who they may have avoided because of drug or alcohol-related mistakes. The later steps in the program focus on attunement and greater attempts to increase one's conscious contact with God, as they understand Him, through the practice of Prayer (Speaking to God) and Meditation (Listening to God). The final steps encourage those who have had a spiritual awakening as a result of these steps to carry this message to others who are still suffering.

Chapter 9

How to Spot It... Signs and Symptoms that you can Look for to Determine if your Loved One is Using Mood-Altering Medications

If you are reading this book, one would think that you already suspect, or have confirmed, that your loved one is using drugs or other mood-altering substances. To help you put more pieces of the puzzle together, I thought it may be beneficial to go over some basic things that you may have noticed, or could look out for in the future, to determine if your loved one is abusing mood-altering substances and possibly even assess the severity of their addiction.

Before we proceed, I think it is important that you take the blame off yourself for not noticing sooner some of the things we will discuss in this chapter. The nature and inherent characteristics of substance abuse typically contain concealment of behaviors, including the expenditure of money and unexplained disappearances at random times. Please take a moment to think about all of the excuses and seemingly irrational tales your loved one may have told you up to this point. To be completely honest, your loved one may still actually believe these tales they are telling you. Recovery literature states at some point in one's descent into addiction, the addict literally reaches a point where they cannot differentiate the true from the false.

I think that it is also important to note that your loved one may have developed Antisocial Personality Disorder traits as they have proceeded beyond the early stages of addiction. As suggested elsewhere in this book, given the fact that addiction hijacks the instinctual regions of the brain, the goal or primary target for an addict becomes feeding the addiction. That means that your loved one will utilize any means necessary, including lying and stealing, to feed the addiction. It does not mean that your loved one does not love you, or that they are trying to hurt you intentionally. Given the fact that you are connected to the addict by heartstrings of love, you have simply placed yourself in a more vulnerable position, willing to give him/her the benefit of the doubt more so than most others in his/her life.

So, what have you observed thus far? Many alcohol and drug awareness prevention programs highlight various things to consider. Signs of addiction include the following: your loved one speaking of or hanging out with new friends; abandonment of former friends; engaging in new activities; listening to new bands or types of music; changing clothing styles; coming into new sources of money or electronics; not being able to account for the expenditure of their funds; changes in their typical sleep/wake cycle; attitudinal or dispositional changes; changes in skin tone or having more acne or unexplained rashes or bumps; differences in body odor or types of cologne or perfume used; changes in sports team affiliations; different hairstyles and possible weight gain or loss; not wanting to be responsible or accountable for anything; changes in or loss of job; difficulties in their relationships including with their significant other; differences in ways of speaking or language such as utilizing more slang or profane words; ceasing of spiritual or religious practices including not attending services; legal or financial difficulties arising; receiving concerned comments or calls from others close to your loved one who may have a more objective view than yourself; decrease in academic performance or reduction of extracurricular activities; money missing; credit or debit cards misplaced; items disappearing from the home especially electronics or jewelry; inquiring about your maiden name or social security number (to aid in opening a line of credit); avoidance of family functions or social get-togethers; increased blaming or finger-pointing towards yourself or others to take the spotlight off themselves; increased accusations of how things that happened in the past are causing their current change in behavior; avoidance of making eye contact; clammy or cold to the touch; more frequent trips to the physician or hospital for either pill seeking or to treat a host of respiratory issues or other infections that could arise as a result of drug use; changes in dating or sexual behavior including increased promiscuity; making empty promises; not living up to their word; and others, but this list should suffice for now.

I could have kept going, but I just wanted to illuminate the fact that the signs may be pronounced or subtle. I would advise that you inquire about any of these behaviors with your loved one if you have not done so already. To be effective in your appeal and to be of assistance to your loved one, I encourage that you examine your tone and style of communication. If you are reading this book, likely there have already been several unpleasant interactions with a very heated exchange of words. This is not helpful to either party involved.

I will simply ask that you make the best of this opportunity to be of influence by not nagging, threatening, criticizing, or complaining about your loved one to their face. This simply increases the emotional space between the two of you and demotes you from a position of being a positive influence in their life. Additionally, your loved one is most likely carrying more guilt and shame than you could imagine. You may not easily detect the guilt and shame because the actual drug use is covering it up in a perpetual cycle of addiction.

If you can keep your intellect intact and your emotional reaction under control, you will fare much better in your attempt to relay your care and concern to your loved one. Approach them with the acceptance and understanding that you would devote to a person dying with a terminal illness. Please note, I am not setting you up to be swindled or for further enabling. The rest of this book asserts to not enable by illuminating the characteristics to look out for and how not to be codependent. Yet, it is important that if your intuitive sense and gut tell you that your loved one is in a more receptive mood to hear your concern, then this may not be the time for more "tough love" techniques.

A change in your communication pattern will elicit a change in theirs as well. Ideally, your nonjudgmental and unconditional love and acceptance of them will have your loved one be more receptive to your support. This may be difficult for you, given your own frustration and hurt, but I suggest that you find a trusted professional therapist or counselor to discuss these issues. You do not want to unintentionally cause further harm or distance in your relationship with your loved one.

The fact that you are reaching out for professional assistance, via therapy or counseling, may alert your loved one to the true gravity of the situation, which may also work in your (and his/her) favor in the long run. It most certainly would not harm you to discuss your hurt and frustration in a therapeutic setting, while being offered understanding and guidance from a reputable professional. Therapy could help diffuse your emotional reaction, and possibly help you take a more strategic role in assisting your loved one.

Chapter 10
Treat Them as Adults... if They Are

Are you ready for some shocking truth and honesty? Hold on...get ready, and here you go. Stop doing what you are doing for your loved one if they are able to do these things on their own. If they are above the age of 18 years old, and do not suffer from severe or persistent mental health issues, or have a cognitive disability that limits their understanding, let them handle their business. I have heard many family members complain in exasperation about what they must do to ensure that their loved one's needs are met. They complain about having to provide transportation, buying food, providing childcare, bailing them out, finding them jobs, paying for their housing, ensuring that they have clean clothes, reminding them of appointments, and a host of other time costing and precious resource-robbing activities. The family member's heart is in the right place, but unfortunately, their mindset is significantly off course.

Pulling back from helping your loved one meet daily life needs may seem counterintuitive. Your first question may be, how will all of these things get done? Admittedly, some, if not many, of these items will be moved to the back burner. I am not suggesting that you let the children of these individuals suffer, by any means. If the adult who has a substance abuse problem is not able to meet the conditions necessary to raise his/her children, then please step in (legally) and take over custody. Legal custody will afford you benefits for providing for these children. If you are not able to do this, please, I urge you, contact the Department of Social Services. The Department of Social Services can open a case to ensure the child's (or children's) welfare is protected. By no means am I suggesting that you should allow children to experience abuse or neglect. Any suspicions of child abuse or neglect should be reported to law enforcement authorities or the Department of Social Services as soon as you are aware of such instances.

Outside of the issue of children, please let your loved one fall flat on his/her face if they should not meet the responsibilities of being an adult because of their addiction. The longer you come to the rescue, the further you enable their dependence. The more you do, the less they will do. The law of diminishing returns does not support your continued efforts.

Remember that your loved one has one sole focus and concern, selfishly feeding their addiction by any means necessary. Money to them is calculated by how much of a particular alcoholic beverage or drug they will be able to purchase using that money, and for how long it will keep them high. They are not concerned about your retirement or their children's future educational fund while they are at the height of their addiction. The sooner you grasp this concept, the less you will spend needlessly in your attempt to help them.

Allowing a loved one to actually become homeless, does not make you a bad person. Permitting your loved one to remain in jail until the judge says otherwise, will not make you a terrible person. Refusing to pay an addict's bills, will not ruin your credit (unless the bill is in your name because no one else would give them a line of credit). Ensuring that their children are protected through legal and social services will give the children of addicts the best opportunity to have a typical childhood. Continuing to foster dependence simply allows the addiction to saturate and taint any sparse hope of having a normal existence.

I say this all in a loving manner. I know this is hard. I felt that I needed to shake you up a little with the blunt truth to shift you into a strategic mindset. Remember, your best efforts have led you to read this book. Please be open to a new way of operating, that is all I ask. Take a moment to reflect on all of the things that you have done for your loved one that they could have done for themself. Can you see how your efforts to support your loved one could actually exacerbate the problems of addiction by making it easier for him/her to continue to use drugs or alcohol?

You may need to consult with a therapist or mental health professional about appropriate ways that you can begin taking a different approach. I urge you to take steps to ensure your safety, first and foremost. If there has ever been any violence or aggression exhibited by your loved one, even threats, please take the appropriate measures to ensure your safety. When you cut a loved one off, they may have an overly harsh reaction. They may say things like "You don't love me," or they may find other ways to shift the blame for their miserable life to you. Your loved one may highlight your own shortcomings in an attempt to guilt you and shame you back into assisting them in the manner that they prefer. They may be quite mean and hurtful.

If they threaten you, contact law enforcement immediately. These threats may be idle, but I want you to demonstrate to your loved one that you will not back down. You will not succumb to these types of manipulation or control tactics anymore. I stress that you assess your safety, and their potential emotional reaction, when you begin to put these principles of tough love into action. Your loved one, who is dependent upon a substance, suffers from a mental impairment that will cloud his/her best judgment. You are not dealing with the apple of your eye anymore, even though the images of them as innocent and precious infants may still be fresh in your mind. You are now dealing with their addiction...the beast or other personality that simply wants to get its next fix at any cost.

Once you decide to take this "tough love" course of action, there is no turning back or modifying any of the new terms of your relational agreement, unless YOU deem this fitting. Bargaining or negotiating with your loved one, silently translates to him/her that manipulation and control are still possible. Be firm and resolute. This is the way it is, and this is the way it has to be.

Your new attitude and stance will be tested. Prepare yourself. Their behaviors may even become more exaggerated in an attempt to soften your resolve. The threat of harm to themselves or others may be voiced...Call 911 or law enforcement immediately if self-harm threats are voiced. I repeat, if your loved one threatens to harm or kill themselves or anyone else, CALL 911 IMMEDIATELY!

This is not the time to take their threats lightly. Their fragility and compromised psychological state will be further compromised by their funding or transportation resource (YOU) terminating their unwritten contractual agreement. The new rules will be upsetting to them, to say the least. Give it a couple of days. They may never wish to speak to you again, as they probably have already threatened this once in the past to manipulate you into doing for them what they could have done for themselves.

Are you ready to enact a plan? Take some time to consider what needs to be done, and another moment to anticipate their reaction. Pre-plan your responses to their likely emotional reactions. Do not deviate from this course of action. The more you plan for their reactions, including utilizing the assistance from another family member or friend who can serve as a witness and possibly keep a situation from getting worse, the better the potential outcome. Please note: this conversation does not have to be done face to face. However, utilizing a cell phone may end up with you getting hung up on, followed by a barrage of unkind and possibly threatening text messages. If the text messages are threatening, again, please contact law enforcement authorities to proceed with a proper course of action to reduce this type of behavior. Your loved one may even need to be incarcerated.

Now, I am not wishing that your loved one gets placed in jailed or committed to a hospital for a psychological evaluation. However, I would not argue against this either if it is needed. Being detained under the appropriate supervision of a hospital or jail could help bring clarity to your loved one regarding the gravity of their situation. Being incarcerated or held for a 72-hour psychological evaluation, will temporarily suspend their ability to abuse any substance. Being placed in either of these institutions may bring the onset of withdrawal, and they will most likely be past the acute stages of withdrawal by the time of release or discharge. For this reason, incarceration or being held for a psychological evaluation may present a new beginning for all involved.

It is important to understand that addicts, especially opiate and heroin addicts, will go to any lengths to avoid withdrawal. Having sex for money or drugs, stealing, robbing, writing fraudulent checks, or simply using all of their savings to get their drug is not uncommon for these individuals. I want to share a brief version of a police report that I read in our local paper a few years ago.

The police report stated that a man walked into a local pharmacy store and proceeded directly to the pharmacy counter. He handed the pharmacy tech a note stating that he wanted her to give him all of the "Roxi & Oxi" that the pharmacist had, referring to the opioid pain pills Roxicodone® & Oxycodone®. He stated that he had a gun. The police report continued by saying that the pharmacy tech complied with his request, gave him a bag with the prescription pills he requested, and the man left the store without further incident.

I want to illustrate a singleness of purpose or mindset here. The assailant is facing "25 years to Life" in prison for Armed Robbery if apprehended. Facing this lengthy sentence, the assailant did not ask for money from the register, a pack of cigarettes, or even a Snicker's bar. I would assume that the assailant was in the mid to late stages of opiate/opioid withdrawal and he was simply willing to do whatever it takes to avoid the pain of further withdrawal symptoms.

Please consider this story when thinking about your maneuvers to take a new strategy with your loved one. If incarceration or hospital commitment happens to arise, well, I would argue the temporary upset to their life would be less than 25 years to life in prison.

Getting your loved one separated from their beloved drug of choice is an important first step. Your influence in their life through your actions is all you have. You cannot control their behavior, as you most certainly have recognized by this point. So please stop attempting to do so and find ways to utilize your influence to shape their behavior in a healthier direction.

The theory of the stick and carrot resurfaces as you are free to commit to providing them resources (within healthy limits) to take the steps they need to embrace their recovery. If they tell you that you don't love them or you would otherwise be assisting them in whatever manner that they would like, you can kindly remind them that you would be happy to help if they are willing to get sober and embrace recovery. When they tell you of their plan to do this in the next week, month, or decade, gently remind them that they can then and only then request any further assistance from you, after having made this step into recovery. When they reel off the reasons why they cannot start recovery efforts today, simply tell them that your intuitive spirit has made up its mind and that you are unwilling to assist their demise any further.

Chapter 10

Please prepare yourself psychologically, emotionally, and physically to endure an onslaught of the lewdest and most vulgar words that you may have ever heard from your loved one. Please know that you may just be saving their life, and I will argue strongly that you will be improving your life, regardless of the outcome.

Chapter 11
Fear of Failure vs Fear of Success

You may be wondering why would anyone fear success? Well... inspirational author Marianne Williamson stated that "Our deepest fear is not that we are inadequate. Our deepest fear is that we are powerful beyond measure. It is our Light, not our Darkness, that most frightens us." Ponder this statement for a moment before continuing.

Now, go on a journey with me inside the recesses of the mind of the loved one whom you have cared for and cried over for years. Please take a moment to see the world as they do. Remember that perception is an individual process. Think about the experiences that they have been through, and what they have dealt with and endured (in their conscious and lucid moments). Think about how they have felt when they have subjected themselves to the sordid life and affairs that are the underbelly of mid to late stages of addiction. Don't skip over the unmentionables either.

I had heard a lady speak at a recovery meeting early in my sobriety and she shared that people looked at her with a mixture of pity and disgust. I immediately identified with this statement, though I would not have been able to verbalize it as succinctly at that stage of my recovery. I am still able to recall the glares and down-turned faces that passed me by on the streets of Downtown Charleston, South Carolina, as I wandered disheveled and aimlessly at the low point of my own addiction. Yes, this was near my bottom, though I had a couple more unsuccessful years of attempting to keep drinking and using drugs before God used a proverbial sledgehammer to crumble my reliance upon self-will.

I share my personal story to help you understand that the pits of addiction create more shame and guilt in your loved one than your comments could ever create. I also want to assist you in developing more compassion and empathy, not sympathy, for your loved one. Finding compassion for your loved one should diminish your frustration. Your frustration level is inversely proportional to your compassion and empathy levels. Increase one, the other goes down. You choose which is more beneficial to all parties involved.

Back to the insight shared in Williamson's quote; your loved one (and others) may find comfort and complacency in his/her misery and may not be able to muster the necessary motivation to break out of this addiction pattern. He/she may be stuck with a limited scope or understanding of the true preciousness of life unless he/she has a spiritual awakening and/or receives professional help. Your loved one likely feels totally hopeless when not impaired or high. Addiction makes it impossible to imagine a world where they could look others in the eye and shake hands as equals. Attempting to be "normal" is more frightening than the what the AA Big Book refers to as a "certain sense of security in the familiar" within the drug-infested, criminally charged cesspool that is their current reality.

A core aspect of addiction from an intrapsychic level, is that addiction corrupts internally before the full effects are seen externally. Every shaming behavior by the addict further erodes the sunlight of the spirit and dulls the inner voice that guides most of us. Addiction hijacks the core centers of the brain, takes control, and like malware, infects and taints all memory files. Normal processing becomes obsolete. It is simply too much for an addicted person who has abdicated responsibility, shunned accountability, and has allowed all things that possess meaning and purpose to slip away.

If you now have a better glimpse of the world your loved one lives in, you may have a greater understanding of how they could fear success.

How could they ever attain a high position in work or society after all of the low-life things they have done? Who would ever want to be with them or love them after they have turned their back and hurt so many close to them? What would they do with a spotlight on them to shine on all of their defects of character? Why would anyone ever trust them again? When would they ever be able to get past their current chaotic crisis to begin moving forward in life?

These are difficult questions to face head on and there are not any simple answers. The answers began to unfold as one accepts that his/her journey through addiction and into recovery may just be their most important life lesson. The Big Book of AA states that "we will not regret the past nor wish to shut the door on it." This concept brings us to our next point.

Most people are familiar with the concept of reincarnation, regardless of their faith or religion. Please consider for a moment that your loved one will experience a sort of reincarnation or rebirth, should they remain sober and in recovery. The lifestyle of the addict is one that is in complete contrast to the lifestyle of an individual in recovery. I have heard that "you only have to change ONE thing to stay sober and in recovery...and that one thing is EVERY-THING."

To tie together these assertions, your loved one's journey into addiction will provide the bedrock for them to amass their recovery efforts. I am not suggesting that this transition will happen on their first attempt into sobriety, or in their first month of abstinence. However, the recovery groups do assist in giving a person who feels their life is absent of meaning, a sense of purpose and some life direction. As Alcoholics Anonymous states, "Our primary purpose is to stay sober and help other alcoholics (or addicts) to achieve sobriety." This is a profound new sense of importance and meaning for those who are fortunate enough to make it to the recovery rooms of AA or NA.

I hope that as we have spoken about the difficulty in self-concept and self-esteem that your loved one may be struggling with, that your sense of compassion has increased, if only incrementally. One cannot be peaceful and resentful at the same time. I encourage you to take a moment, or even several minutes each day, to pray and/or meditate for your loved one's well-being. Briefly recall the terror that they may be dealing with in the height of their addiction and pray for their redemption from this affliction.

Your loved one who is struggling will not be able to readily accept the truth that their life can be wonderful, and those miraculous events will unfold if they trust God and stay sober. In the recovery rooms, the word miracle is quite often heard regarding individuals who are able to get sober and stay in recovery. While this may sound a little sappy, it is quite appropriate. One author defines a miracle as simply something that defies the laws of nature. For an Alcoholic not to drink or an Addict not to use, well, this is truly a miracle as defined.

Chapter 12
Limbic Resonance and Neurochemical Imbalance

You may have noticed that you are attracted to, or have become friends with, the same "kind of people" over the course of your life. We could allude to the spiritual meaning or soul significance behind these synchronistic meetings, but for the sake of this chapter (and book), I will attempt to explain this phenomenon by another means. It is termed limbic resonance. Limbic resonance refers to the fact that the limbic region of the brain is activated when we encounter things or people that have some sort of familiarity that evoke deep emotional states. It can also refer to the energetic exchange between two people offering a sense of compatibility with some people, or an emotional hijacking with others.

The limbic region of the brain and the limbic system is a group of forebrain structures that includes the hypothalamus, the amygdala, and the hippocampus. These brain components are involved in motivation, emotion, learning, and memory. The limbic system is located where the subcortical structures meet the cerebral cortex.

Limbic resonance suggests that the capacity for sharing deep emotional states arises from the limbic system of the brain. These states include the dopamine-circuitry which promotes feelings of empathic harmony, and the norepinephrine- circuitry originating emotional states such as fear, anxiety, and anger. This circuitry explains why you may have had an almost instantaneous attraction to your life-long partner, or why you may have had similar types of friends over the course of your life. Limbic resonance also explains familiarity and nostalgic feelings that arise in certain places and over certain objects and smells.

I have only discussed the positive factors associated with limbic resonance thus far, but unfortunately, it also explains why your loved one may appear to be attracted to people, places, or things that are unhealthy and potentially dangerous. When dopamine is involved, we are talking about the pleasure and reward pathway driving motivation. Dopamine is the reason we like ice cream, a hug, and cocaine. "It feels good, do it again" is the mantra of dopamine. Sex, drugs, and Rock-n-Roll all activate the pleasure-reward pathway. Consider that crystal methamphetamine has been shown to be exponentially more powerful and rewarding than good sex from a neurochemical perspective. Now you may understand the reason addiction is referred to as a brain disease.

The Food and Drug Administration (FDA), which is responsible for approving pharmaceuticals and maintaining the safety and quality of what we ingest for nutrition, is housed under the same roof for a specific reason. Any substance we ingest, food or drug, can have an effect on the chemicals in our body and on the neurochemicals in our brain. Now you understand why your favorite treat (i.e. cheesecake, crème brûlée, or Oreos) have such a powerful force over finding their way into your mouth and tummy. It is not the drug, but the effect that the drug has on neurochemicals and neurotransmitters in the brain, which is primarily responsible for your loved one's addiction. You are not to blame.

The limbic resonance phenomenon is also why your loved one is attracted to certain types of individuals and environments. Those people and places are simply rewarding and familiar. For this reason, recovery attempts are even harder when individuals are still surrounded by others with former drug-using associations. This understanding is what leads me to my personal belief and reasoning behind my suggestions and recommendations supporting inpatient treatment or sober housing options for those early in recovery. This brain and limbic resonance phenomenon can simply overwhelm any individual's self-will at times, especially in times of stress and discomfort (as seen in the early withdrawal phases and the early stages of recovery).

The limbic response can be reversed or reset gradually, but it requires attempts to delay gratification and short-term rewards. Short-term rewards are important while working toward longer-term rewards, which require greater effort before being reinforced.

A change in "people, places, and things" can disrupt this reinforcement schedule. If your loved one is able to seek inpatient services or sober housing, this may allow for them to start gradually replacing and replenishing a holistically healthier and greater life promoting reward and pleasure reinforcement schedule. Cessation from their current drug seeking behaviors and subsequent reinforcements from dopamine will leave your loved one "irritable, restless, and discontent". It is vital that they develop a plan of recovery or that this is attended to in the early days of abstinence from their drug of choice if they are to be successful.

Chapter 13

What to do if your Loved One Reaches out for Help... The Basics

If your loved one reaches out for help, please assess their level of sincerity, and make sure that this is not simply another veiled attempt to manipulate you out of additional resources. If they pass your acid test, then promptly and calmly help your loved one identify the options available. This may require the assistance of a physician or emergency room to ensure their physical and medical safety.

If your loved one has been taking benzodiazepines (i.e. Xanax®, Valium®, Klonopin®, Ativan®) and/or drinking alcohol on a daily basis, please do not skip this vital step of getting medical assistance immediately. Given that withdrawal from central nervous system depressants can be FATAL, it is imperative that your loved one gets to a medical setting to evaluate their withdrawal potential and associated risks. A medical professional can help determine the potential for such risks and develop a plan for your loved one to be safely tapered off the substance.

It also would be wise to have your loved one seen by a physician, or medical provider, regardless of his/her drug of choice, if they decide to stop using. Other medical conditions (i.e. high blood pressure, diabetes, cardiovascular issues, or respiratory issues) could be exacerbated by withdrawal symptoms. It is also unlikely that your loved one was appropriately treating or taking medications for such conditions while in the peak of his/her addiction stages.

Attending to their medical needs may also include a visit to a physician for other medications that can assist and bolster recovery efforts. Lack of sleep is a typical complaint from folks who are in the acute, or post-acute, withdrawal stage. There are several non-habit-forming medications that could assist with restoring sleep, such as Trazodone® (please have him/her consult their physician about this of course, as I am not an MD or DO).

If your loved one has been previously diagnosed with any other mental health disorders (i.e. Depression, Anxiety, Bipolar Disorder, and other Mood Dysregulation Issues), getting him/her stabilized on appropriate mental health prescriptions will be a vital first step to achieving psychological and emotional stability.

I will assert that I have seen many individuals early in recovery benefit from a simple antidepressant (SSRI) prescription. Alcohol and drug use change the neurochemistry in the brain, meaning that it alters the levels of neurotransmitters like Serotonin, Dopamine, GABA, Glutamate, Norepinephrine, and others. One can achieve a greater sense of wellness much more quickly with the utilization of antidepressant medications. Antidepressant medications can restore the chemical imbalance of the brain more quickly than waiting on the natural process of restoration to occur by the brain and body on their own, especially in the early stages of recovery.

It is wise to make sure existing mental health issues and disorders are attended to in the early stages of recovery. Issues such as Bipolar Disorder or Anxiety can be safely and effectively treated with medication. Treating underlying mental health issues will allow a person to feel stabilized and more comfortable in their own skin. Addressing these other mental health disorders will also potentially reduce the risk of substance use or relapse, especially if your loved one had attempted to use illicit substances to mood alter to treat these underlying issues as part of their own self-medicating strategies.

Chapter 14

Numbing Vulnerability... and All Other Feelings Incidentally

When discussing the core reasons why people use drugs and alcohol to excess, it is important to highlight the issue of vulnerability. Brené Brown introduced the concept of vulnerability and wholehearted living into the mainstream during her Ted Talk years ago, and subsequent appearances on Oprah's network (OWN™). Brené Brown clearly demonstrated that many people use substances and maladaptive behaviors to numb feelings of vulnerability. Brown also clearly states that by doing so, the substance abuser, unfortunately, ends up numbing all of his/her feelings, including the good stuff (joy, gratitude and happiness).

I mention Brené Brown and her work on vulnerability to encourage you to follow up on her other publications and videos. I feel reviewing Brown's work is a compelling way to assist you in understanding your loved one's dilemma, and why he/she may emotionally turn to their drug of preference for relief.

Based on Brown's research and a greater understanding of the implications of vulnerability, we find that we are a society simply not "feeling good enough." We feel like we are not good enough for a variety of reasons including not being thin enough, rich enough, tall enough, and other stereotypes the media glamorizes. Brown mentions that we fall into the ever-vicious cycle of numbing our vulnerability with drugs, feeling bad, then numbing again. After repeated exposure or daily use, our world becomes null and void of joy. Once simple pleasures are hidden under the layers of misery and pain. We become sensitive to the upwelling of emotions that still happens while impaired, but the negative feelings are numbed. This impairs the normal functioning of the individual in ever greater capacities until finally, the only source of peace is offered by the impairment a drug provides. The catch-22 of drug use is that it is only a temporary feeling or numbing.

Exploring vulnerability is not at the top of most people's priority list, as it is usually quite the contrary. Most people avoid vulnerability like the plague. We tend to associate vulnerability with weakness and a sense of being exposed. The reason for this discussion of vulnerability is to increase your capacity for understanding your loved one. I also challenge you to explore your own concept and understanding of how you too may avoid feeling or being vulnerable.

Providing a safe, loving, and warm place for your loved one, or providing an ear for your loved one to vent, is not antithetical to my previous discussion on tough love. Actually, it is how I would encourage you to enact your tough love approach, guided by this new understanding of your loved one's situation. Recognizing a desperate cry for help, versus a manipulative ploy for plunging for more resources, can only be recognized by you or a trained mental health professional. Your ability to distinguish between these two polar opposite motives could save their life and your retirement savings.

Brené Brown routinely asks her audience or participants to fill in the blank of the following statement: "I am not _____ enough!" I want you to try to fill in the blank with at least the first three words or phrases that pop into your mind. Was this hard? I doubt it, unless you just finished an hour of mindfulness-based yoga or meditation, while overlooking a tranquil Zen Garden.

Now I ask that you attempt to fill in the blank for your loved one. Keep going until you come up with at least ten responses to fill in the blank. Multiply this by 10 or 100 and you may now have a clearer sense of the sense of defeat that your loved one struggles with shaking each day.

Chapter 15
The Family... Onwards and Upwards...

So, let's say all goes well and your loved one is able to seek treatment and maintain some semblance of an early recovery experience. Well, now what? Celebrate? Interrogate? Not yet. This is just the beginning of a lifelong process. For both the loved one in recovery, the other affected family members, and you. You may be asking why we should delve into this topic once again since the book has been mostly about this issue anyway.

Well, I think that it is important to review why you have been holding on and hanging around your loved one as long as you have been, despite his/her unhealthy behaviors and the impact they have had on your life. You have tolerated late-night phone calls, incessant demands that emotional or financial needs be met, and all other sorts of ridiculous behavior up until this point. So, what is going to stop you from continuing to tolerate similar antics, disguised with the mask of sobriety and recovery?

It is vital that you, and your family, read, research, or seek professional resources, including a therapist and/or other support groups to assist with navigating these early stages of recovery. You need to begin to recognize the signs and symptoms of irresponsibility, and the shedding of accountability that your loved one in recovery may hide behind. Please do not expect your loved one to be able to resume a life full of responsibility and accountability in the first weeks of their sobriety. That is not what I am proposing. However, your loved one should be able to get to work or make provisions to do so, on their own, by this time. They should be able to wake themselves up in the morning, keep a calendar of their appointments, and keep commitments, without being reminded by you or others, of their need to attend these events.

Your loved one should assume financial responsibility for his/her life and debts. Bailing them out at this stage, even though they are sober, is questionable, as it sets up a shadow of possibility in their mind that you will continue to come to the rescue. Using a money match program, similar to an employer's 401k program, is the most you should consider at this point, in terms of support. Buying them a new car... "so they can get to work," would undermine the consequences of their past decisions. I am not recommending that you allow your loved one to become homeless and fend for himself/herself on the streets in early recovery if they have accepted some of your suggestions up until this point. You do not want to place them at risk for violence or other unmentionable acts. I would say to invest your dollars in placing them in a transitional program or other sober housing option. This is a better living option at this stage of recovery versus paying for a one-bedroom, secluded apartment and accepting lease terms on their behalf. Living alone could cause the recovering individual to feel loneliness and a sense of isolation which are relapse triggers.

What I am attempting to highlight, is that your attempt to help will need outside or objective feedback from others, well versed in the disease of addiction, to keep you from unintentionally (of course) sabotaging their recovery efforts. I also want to add a layer of protection for you because the debates and challenges to their requests for assistance will be quite heated. They may attempt to manipulate you and even threaten to start drinking or using again. If so, let them. It is their life, not yours. They may attempt to guilt you into believing their ploy that their life was better when using, and perhaps, they may be sort of right if they never had to face typical life responsibilities and take accountability for their behavior (at least from their unhealthy perspective at this point).

If you have always come to the rescue and funded all sorts of unknown sordid affairs (unknowingly), then life will likely be more challenging for them sober. The purpose of this book is to equip and enable you with some basic knowledge to prevent you from falling victim to these ploys. I want to help assist you in helping your loved one navigate the recovery journey in the most successful manner possible.

My encouragement to you is to ask yourself serious questions before coming to the aid of your loved one. Why are they not able to handle or deal with this situation with their own resources? Offer to provide them information on resources or other things that may be of service to them before making the phone calls on their behalf. Ask them what specifically they need from you, besides money, and offer ways that you are willing to assist, besides giving them cash.

It is important to break the codependent and enabling cycles that had formed over the years of their addiction. This is the first step in restoring balance to the family system. Other children and loved ones have taken a lesser priority, unintentionally, as the addict's repeated crises always took the top spot in daily conversations and actions. This left others to feel as if their life and contributions were not valued or respected at times.

Restoring a proper and healthy balance is the key to achieving holistic health for the family. I have worked with a family who opted to not attend one of their daughter's graduation from college as they felt it was more important to provide surveillance of their other adult daughter who was in an outpatient program and living out of state. Their comments about this were more concerning, as they simply stated that the daughter who was graduating from college would understand as this type of thing has happened for years as their irresponsible drug-addicted daughter always had a way of interrupting important family events and holidays. The wrong behavior is being rewarded unintentionally in my perspective as the responsible daughter again does not benefit from gaining her parents attention and admiration because of the irresponsibility of the daughter in treatment.

Just because these types of instances may be normal in their family (or yours) does not mean that they are typical or representative of a healthy family system functioning optimally. I would encourage you to examine some of the previous dynamics in your relationships and family, and identify where you see an imbalance of time, attention, and resources given to one family member over others.

It is important for you to be honest about truly how much of an impact and possible investment of time and resources you have bestowed on your loved one with a substance use disorder. After taking or making this honest appraisal, you may be more equipped with the appropriate motivation to take the necessary steps forward for you, your family, and your loved one's best interest.

Chapter 16
Just the Facts, Please...
Just the Facts

Please, do not attempt to scare or threaten your loved one into receiving help. Many addicts and alcoholics have become emboldened by this approach by others, including: Judges, probation officers, bosses, etc.... Your threats or attempts to connect via this approach to your loved one will deafen your pleas to your loved one. You are probably correct in your stated concerns, but your loved one has built a wall of resistance to this approach to maintain their addiction.

Remember that your loved one at times lives in a fantasy world of delusion. They will use their substance use and abuse, and associated drug seeking behaviors, as an attempt to blot out the reality of their situation. Being cognizant of their delusional thinking will help you proceed with greater levels of success. Your loved one knows that they could go to jail, hurt or injure someone, lose everything, or die; but they are quite sure that this will not happen to them.

I suggest that simply and nonchalantly presenting the facts of their situation will garner you, and them, greater dividends. Reminding them of how their behavior has directly brought about their negative consequences may be helpful. This is because most addicts will avoid the blame for creating any unpleasant situations in their life at all costs, through psychological defense mechanisms. Avoiding accountability and responsibility becomes an art form by the moderate stages of the progression of their addiction.

Highlighting the medical, financial, and legal quandaries that may arise, or have arisen, due to their substance use is useful. Limit the judgmental tone, as your loved one will tune you out. Most folks who suffer from alcohol or drug addiction will have moments of clarity, however brief, and a few sincere factual concerns will chip away at their disease's guarded defenses. Figuring these times out may rely on your intuitive senses, but it may not be immediately following a calamity. Waiting a day or so, and then approaching them with a simple invite for a meal or other outing, could provide you this space.

Being sincere about their well-being, holding back your anger and disappointment with their current state of affairs, and offering amiable and acceptable alternatives is a better route to achieve success. Constant harping or nagging will push them away from you, and your opportunity for being a positive influence will dissipate. Approach them in a peaceful manner where they will not be able to deny your love and concern. Allowing them the freedom of choice (if they are over 18 years old) will show them that you respect them and simply want what is best for them.

You may need to do some research on the Surgeon General's Report on the Role of Addiction in our nation that was published in 2016 (go to my website for a web link to this). For the first time, the head of our medical field chose to lay out the pressing concerns that face our nation and families, as it concerns the risks and impacts of addiction. Discussing prior family members who have struggled with addiction or alcoholism, highlights the genetic linkage of the disease. Genetic predisposition to addiction and alcoholism has been verified by the medical professionals. Research has indicated that those who have such predispositions are four times more likely to develop problems with alcohol or drugs, than those who do not have such.

Also, factors such as ethnicity, the age of first use, and reported high levels of tolerance, are important. Certain ethnicities are more or less prone to developing problems with various substances, due to genetics and enzymes which process the substance in the body. It has been shown that the age at which a person first uses a drug or begins to drink alcohol on a regular basis also affects the potential severity of the addiction problem over the course of that individual's life. Typically, the sooner that a person first uses a drug, or begins using on a regular basis, will cause them to evidence far greater problematic use over the course of their life than those who pick up the substance later in life.

Tolerance is an interesting factor. Most individuals feel that having a high tolerance is a protective factor, but this is an erroneous thought. Individuals that exhibit a high tolerance typically have more of the enzyme that breaks down the substance of choice. Again, this is a genetic issue, but our culture is one where those who can hold their liquor are celebrated and using high doses or large amounts of various illicit substances is seen as representative of an individual's superiority or coolness. One can easily understand the detrimental effects of how this can quickly be turned into a deficit that prompts them ever so closer to passing into the realms of addiction.

Breathalyzers were placed in bars and restaurants for a short period of time several years ago, to assist patrons with knowing whether they were too impaired to drive home given their state's accepted legal limits regarding BAC or BAL (alcohol levels in the bloodstream) for driving an automobile. This safety measure was quickly abused by certain groups of patrons to see how high they could get their blood alcohol level in comparison with friends. Again, those with higher tolerances would be able to exceed the legal limit several times over and let us hope they did not get behind the wheel of a car.

Speaking of tolerance regarding alcohol, most folks without a high tolerance to alcohol would not be able to get to the various states' legal limits and still be able to even attempt to operate a car. Those individuals who exceed the legal limit for impaired driving offenses by double or more (typically greater than 0.15 BAC or BAL) in most circumstances show evidence of high tolerance. For a non-drinker, attempting to get close to 0.15 BAC or BAL would most likely result in them passing out. Yet for those who have a greater genetic tolerance, their best game of pool or coolest dance moves may not come until they reach these levels.

This brings us to blackouts, or periods of time where an individual simply does not recall the events that had transpired the previous evening. Most individuals will not reach a blackout unless they ingest a large quantity of alcohol (or mix it with benzodiazepines-which can be fatal as mentioned previously) in a very short period of time (doing numerous shots for one's birthday (do you remember your 21st?)). For those who blackout on a semi-frequent basis, this would most likely be representative of having a remarkably high tolerance and evidence of an alcohol use disorder.

Alcohol is a central nervous system depressant. The brain, and its caveman's origin, typically tell the body to go to sleep (pass out) when an individual begins to ingest large amounts of alcohol that impairs the body's ability to function or react to potential threats (saber-tooth tigers). To reach a black-out, an individual must bypass this survival mechanism typically achieved by repeated administrations which increases one's tolerance. Achieving tolerance by bypassing this prehistoric bio-mechanism of survival, an individual is able to walk and function, but the memory centers of the brain are not immune from the effects of the CNS depressant. They simply become impaired, and the short-term memory processes are interrupted.

This tolerance and genetic predisposition can be seen in other classes of drugs as well. Many opiate addicts will report that they "get energy" when taking opioid pain killers or injecting heroin. Many stimulant users of cocaine and "crystal meth" will state that they feel calmer when high. These effects are nearly opposite of the typical physiological effects the drug is stated and created to have on a typical user. Try recalling or asking your loved one what their drug of preference does for them. Listen to their responses.

When speaking of tolerance, it is important to note that physical tolerance increases faster than mental tolerance. This accounts for what we see as functional alcoholics and addicts.

Your body learns to navigate its environment under the influence, with repeated pairings. This explains why certain individuals maintain some level of dexterity and balance after imbibing. Yet, this can fool a person to believing they are not as impaired as they actually are, as mental impairment usually exceeds that of the adaptive physical functions of the body to the ingesting of the preferred substance.

Simply consider how some individuals do not readily appear impaired even though you may detect it through other subtle mechanisms. Reaction times may be significantly delayed, judgment greatly impaired, and motivations subdued. Depending on the substance, remember that impairment is the goal of the drug user, even though they may have learned how to navigate the physical effects and adapted to the more noticeable characteristics, which may cause them to be called out by others.

Now, back to how you may utilize this information to approach your loved one in a more approachable manner. Try these mental exercises to assist which were suggested in the book,

Don't Sweat the Small Stuff and It's All Small Stuff, by Richard Carlson. Look at your loved one and envision them as an infant. Now envision them as an extremely fragile older person. Now, tell them you love them and are here for them if they would like any assistance in restoring their health and relationships. It is okay to describe how you see that their addiction has robbed them of all their inherent gifts and talents. Whether their athletic ability or God-given physical beauty has suffered as a result of their drug use, share with them the beauty and love that you still see residing in them. Their talents, treasures, and gifts may have been dormant for a while, but remind them that they still possess these qualities and will be able to express them as soon as they are able to put down the substance that is taking their life, relationships, and well-being away day-by-day, use-by -use, drink-by-drink.

If you are able to shoot a caring and thoughtful verbal arrow through their addiction's defensive armor, you will have achieved your goal. Remember that the disease of addiction is constantly residing in the recesses of your loved one's mind, repeatedly telling them how worthless they are and how guilty and shameful they should feel. The disease of addiction, and its inner voice, remind them incessantly that they will never be able to acquire anything of value or restore relationships or gain favor from God. The disease of addiction is relentless. So, above all, end your talk with how much you love and care for them, regardless of the direction the conversation takes.

Chapter 17
Now What?

Okay, let us say that your loved one has embraced treatment and is sober for the first time in a long time. You may be wondering how you may best assist them during this time. An entire book could be devoted to this topic, but we will begin with a chapter to give you some diligent information to begin this journey with them.

If your loved one is now sober, regardless of the circumstances that may have led to this, please take a moment to express gratitude for their sobriety and healthy lifestyle decision. They will now have a chance to celebrate life and enjoy the benefits of living a productive and meaningful existence. To be sure, there will be much work to be done to see this process of re-covery to successful fruition.

I have witnessed family members and loved ones put excess pressure on their recovering addict or alcoholic too soon into his/her recov-ery. I am not suggesting that the individual in recovery be given a blank check and not own up for past wrongs or misdeeds, but they will most likely not be able to focus on clearing up the wreckage of their past in a few weeks or even in the first several months of their sobriety. Most importantly, the early stages of recovery are an overly sensitive and delicate period for most in-dividuals in recovery. They will not have the coping skills to fully deal with or handle life on life's terms in the early stages of sobriety.

Remember, that they have been using chem-ical substances to cope with life for a very long time and the naturally occurring coping skills that the typical stages of adult development produces, such as resilience and emotional ma-turity, have eluded them while they were using drugs. They used drugs to go to work, social-ize, deal with stress, sleep, etc... and now they will have to enhance their natural and native coping mechanisms in order to maintain their sobriety.

Most individuals early in recovery will wish to exert greater autonomy in their life. They have been at the beck and call of their drug addiction for such a long period of time that they will enjoy their new sense of freedom, which will most likely irritate those closest to them at times. You may be thinking, well now since they are sober, they can begin to take responsibility for areas of their life that you or others have been assisting or covering while they were on their addicted escapades. You are right to feel that they really should take responsibility for their own lives (and as I have previously suggested), but I am merely suggesting that they may have to break it down into bite-sized increments that they can swallow.

Occasionally, newly sober individuals think they can do everything all at once such as: become gainfully employed; rebuild relationships; take part in children's lives; and keep up with home or domestic duties. However, many

individuals new to recovery will need to maintain some form of recovery program or therapy
to stay on a healthy path. They need to learn the
true definition of self-care and begin practicing
it on a daily basis.

I would suggest encouraging the individual to
take certain responsibilities for his/her own life,
but still be willing to assist and be supportive
of this process. This is not the time to demand
repayment or to hash out the wrongs, hurts,
or harms of the past. Your loved one is simply
not capable of dealing with harsh emotions in
a healthy manner in the early stages of recovery. Making amends to those we have harmed
is Step Nine in the Twelve Step Programs, and
your loved one needs to work through the previous eight steps successfully before commencing
on this ambition.

Most day-to-day tasks and routines will have
to be relearned as they have been managing
these with their drug of choice for years. Going
to the store or a baseball game is a new experience for the newly sober individual. I remember distinctly the moment of confusion I had

when I went to a restaurant for the first time sober. When the server approached the table and asked what I wanted to drink, I truly had to think about my options, as an alcoholic beverage had been my staple for years (I ordered a sweet-tea, being from the South by the way).

These simple and seemingly ordinary day-to-day occurrences are apt to befuddle your newly sober loved one. Adding heavier topics like divorce or death, only compound the feelings of inadequacy in your loved one. I am not suggesting that they should not one day make the proper amends or live in a manner that those who depend on them richly deserve, but becoming overwhelmed and drowning in feelings of inadequacy will not bolster their recovery efforts.

Chapter 18

If You are Married or in a Committed Relationship (with or without children) to the Loved One Struggling with Addiction

If your loved one who suffers from addiction happens to be your partner in life, then any decisions you make regarding his/her addiction will directly impact your own life, understandably. It should be duly noted that not taking any action and allowing the current situation to persist will also directly impact your life.

Regardless of the number of years you share together, we are talking about right now, and about the future of your relationship. If you have children together, things may become more complicated. I hope this chapter will give you some insight on how you can approach your loved one under the various circumstances that may be present within your family system.

I encourage you to have a well thought out plan of action before you decide to implement any suggestions in this book. I understand that you will have to take the financial well-being of your family into consideration as you devise this plan. Every reader's situation will be different, but I hope to convey some general principles that could be applicable across the various situations you may find yourself in.

If children are involved, and custody matters could become a contested issue, I would advise that you seek out legal counsel to find out your rights. Begin documenting things that have transpired, or are transpiring, in your lives, that may need to be presented to a judge one day. I would encourage you to think about your children, and if they are still living at home, what would you ideally like for them to see as a role model in the parent who is currently struggling with addiction. Removing the daily stressors that this person could be causing them, consciously or subconsciously, will most likely benefit their overall well-being, regardless of the pain of having their other parent absent from their lives (hopefully for only a short time period in ideal circumstances).

I am not saying that removing the parent from the home is the only option, but it may be an unfortunate necessary last resort. You will need to begin to get your ducks in a row before you proceed with this step. I would encourage you to consider the additional burdens that may be placed on you regarding childcare and expenses. If you have family members who are willing to assist, please recognize asking them for assistance to promote the well-being of your children should not be seen as groveling for help. Societies and former times where extended family played a dominant role in rearing our children are successful models to replicate. As the saying aptly states, "It takes a village to raise a child."

I would encourage you to take a moment to reflect on how your children may have already been directly or indirectly influenced by their addicted parent's struggles and erratic behaviors. Depending on their age and maturity level, they may have been unable to verbalize these issues to you, as children readily accept their home environment as being completely normal, regardless of the potential dysfunction.

Do they ever have fears or concerns about how their addicted parent's behavior or attitude will be upon arriving home from school? Do they avoid inviting friends over because they are unsure of the state of mind and body their addicted parent will be in? Do they omit school activities or choose not to attend award ceremonies because they feel they may be embarrassed by their addicted parent's interaction with others? These are all relevant concerns that you can bring to the table as you prepare to make the healthiest decisions for you and your family.

I am an advocate for family and marital reconciliation when all parties are in agreement with doing what is necessary to bring health and vitality to the various relationships involved. I am not a fan of allowing children to suffer on behalf of an addicted parent simply because society or religion states that divorce or separation is not an option. In fact, many states have a provision in their legal statutes pertaining to divorce that allow drug addiction or alcoholism to be the sole reason for divorce, which may offer you additional protections (please consult an attorney or lawyer familiar with family law in your state of residence before proceeding).

We all deserve the best life possible but being in a committed relationship with someone dependent on chemicals keeps this from transpiring. Addicts simply usurp the emotional and physical resources that would allow us to experience true contentment. Your loved one's addiction is not their fault, as previously stated, but they do have a decision to make if they wish to keep their family intact. If they choose to embrace sobriety and recovery, support them wholeheartedly, understanding there may be missteps and relapses. If they choose not to take the necessary actions to bring about sobriety and recovery, then I encourage you to take the appropriate steps to promote you and your family's holistic health and well-being.

Many factors will have to be taken into consideration as you depart on this journey. Make a list of things you are willing to accept and things that you are not willing to accept. Become determined to be non-negotiable on these terms if you wish to be successful in your attempt. Once your loved one who is addicted recognizes your fierce determination that they change or your family situation will change, then the onus is on them. Feel free to state the factual reasons why these issues need to be addressed and attempt to avoid emotional reasoning when relaying your requests.

Have some of the facts of life that you have endured together written down and prepared to be presented to them before engaging in this conversation. It will assist you in staying on task and hopefully help in preventing them from deflecting the issue at hand. The issue is their behavior and the subsequent consequences that you and your family have had to live through as a result of their drinking or drug use.

It should be expected that they will dredge up your errors or "wrongful" behaviors in the relationship, which arises simply from an attempt to protect themselves (and their addiction) via their innate defense mechanisms. The goal of this fact sheet is to keep you from falling for the "You don't love me anymore" tactic and to arm you with the steadfast information that will keep you on topic. You can simply reply that you do love them wholeheartedly, but that you are not willing to live in a state of constant chaos and repercussions that their drug use has and is causing in your family and relational life. Simply explain to them that you will not tolerate the uncertainty that their addiction is causing to manifest in your lives together. You have reached your own jumping-off point where a decision must be made by you and them.

Please do not expect an immediate agreement to be made on their part. Allow them to let this conversation sink in and let them chew on what you have just presented. Without knowing the intricacies of your personal relationship, I do not have an estimate on how long it may take for them to come to the realization that either they have to change, or their family or relationship situation is going to change.

Ideally, they will be receptive to the information you presented and take the appropriate actions to get sober by utilizing some of the information in this book. You could assist with lining up a residential treatment program or medication-assisted treatment program that they could call if they would like to take action to get help now. You can say that the fact that you have taken time and energy to find or set up these resources are signs that you do love them and want the best for them.

If they refuse or are unwilling to participate in reaching out for help, well, I encourage you to begin to enact your action plan, after having consulted with your support group and/or attorney. You have a right to live your best life, and so do your children, regardless of your loved one's negative thoughts or comments about this. It is imperative that if you have made this decision, that you hold steady to it and see it through to its completion. Backing down now may only prolong your misery.

Chapter 19

Jails and Institutions... How the Criminal Justice System can be of Assistance

So... the inevitable may have happened or will happen sometime in the future. The pursuit of drugs or obtaining money for drugs may have led your loved one to jail. It is a natural consequence of illegal behavior or activities. It may have brought you embarrassment or concern over your family's reputation. You may have even interpreted this as a blight on your parenting or relational skills. Rest assured, it is their behavior which has led to their incarceration or arrest, and not your lack of appropriate parenting or anything else from your side of the relationship.

Please remember that most of us do the best we can with what we know at any given moment of time. Therefore, with hindsight being 20/20, we can all look back and postulate as to how we could have handled certain situations and relationships better to avoid the mayhem and chaos of the present circumstances. With this guiding your current efforts, release yourself from the bondage of guilt and shame, and allow yourself grace to handle and effectively intervene, to assist your loved one at this current moment in time.

Now, if your loved one should become incarcerated or is arrested for illegal behavior as a result of their addiction, please do not feel that this is the end of the road. It truly may present the new beginning that you have been hoping and praying for. Most municipalities and local court systems have a variety of intervention programs as an option to assist individuals with mental health or substance use disorders. Over 60% of all crime has a traceable component directly to illegal drugs or obtaining money for illicit drugs. Therefore, most court systems have implemented options for the substance-abusing criminal justice-involved populations.

We will discuss a variety of these options to educate you on how you may best guide your loved one through this process. There are Pre-Trial Intervention programs, Drug-Court Programs, Mental Health Courts, Probation & Parole Services, Jail Diversion Programs, and Prison Treatment Programs. I am not an attorney of law and encourage you to consult an attorney or lawyer for specific legal advice on these matters. The following is simply to educate you on what may be available in your area.

Pre-Trial Intervention programs allow a defendant to opt for a program in lieu of going to court. Should the defendant successfully complete the program, usually the charge is dropped, and they are able to get it expunged from their record. This is very advantageous to not impair the future of the individual educationally or vocationally that would result from having a criminal record, but it may only be offered on a one-time basis and only for certain minor or non-violent offenses. As always, please consult an attorney if able, to make sure their rights are protected.

These programs typically involve an intake process after the defendant has accepted this as an option. Rules and regulations are discussed, and the defendant is typically asked to abstain from alcohol and drug use while in the program. Drug screens typically accompany follow-up appointments which may occur once or twice a month. The typical length of the program can vary, with most being 3 to 9 months long. The participant typically must pay for the program and may have to pay restitution if applicable. They are typically required to complete a certain number of community service hours. Occasionally, counseling or therapy may be required, along with a jail tour, and other alcohol & drug education courses.

Drug-Court Programs are typically longer in length and are more intense regarding requirements and treatment. They can range from one to two years in length. These programs sometimes are options for individuals who have felony charges. They typically have various levels of program or treatment intensity with differing degrees of requirements. Most participants are required to get a job, and pay for their group counseling sessions, which may consist of attending three groups a week, along with community support group attendance, such as Alcoholics Anonymous or Narcotics Anonymous. The success of these programs is well documented, but it should be noted that not all participants complete the rigorous requirements, which can skew their numbers regarding success rates. Most defendants must plead guilty to their charge to enter a Drug Court Program. This means that if they do not successfully complete the program, they do not go back to court, but straight to prison if they had a felony offense or were sentenced for a length over six months. Please consult your attorney as to whether this may be the best option for your loved one, as most defendants would prefer this type of program instead of being incarcerated.

The Drug Court Program is a stringent program and will not tolerate non-compliance or successive drug screens that are positive. Therefore, a participant may not appropriately judge their suitability for this type of program or their ability to remain abstinent and end up with a harsh sentence. This is something that your loved one should seriously consider instead of simply looking at this program as a way to avoid incarceration.

If your loved one suffers from co-occurring issues (mental health and substance use diagnoses), you may want to inquire about Mental Health Courts on their behalf. Given that jails and prisons have become the largest mental health institutions in our Country, the legal justice system has implemented a variety of Mental Health Courts to give qualifying offenders the opportunity to avoid incarceration by attending treatment and complying with medication management programs.

These are wonderful alternatives rather than simply incarcerating the individual, without addressing the underlying issues. Mental Health

Courts may have a variety of program components, and you should check on what may be
available in your area.

Jail Diversion Programs and Prison Treatment Programs are also rising in popularity as
a method to reduce recidivism. These programs
typically require a 6 to 12-month commitment
while incarcerated. The offender is an inmate
participant, but typically lives in a separate
housing unit and attends classes, counseling,
and educational sessions throughout the day.
Most of these programs utilize a therapeutic
community approach, where the keys to success
are taking accountability and responsibility for
one's life. They typically have graduated levels
or phases the participant progresses through,
with the higher phased participants assisting
newer participants.

The community is guided by trained staff and
qualified professionals. Some offer transitional
living residences once the participant completes
the program and is released from jail or prison. These programs can be broad in scope, and

participants can spend close to 40 hours per week in scheduled program activities.

Probation & Parole services may also be helpful to assist your loved one to do the right thing. Probation may be offered in lieu of jail time, and having this legal element hanging over your loved one may increase their willingness to participate. Your loved one may strive to stay sober to avoid revocation and possible jail time.

Probation & Parole Agencies typically ask their participants to attend appointments once or twice a month, get a job, take random drug screens, and pay restitution. They can be helpful in guiding participants to vocational or educational services that may assist with other issues that they may be dealing with. Parole Services are similar but typically are offered or required on the tail end of a prison sentence.

Chapter 20
Maintaining Healthy Boundaries

It is quite easy to blur the line of imposing healthy boundaries with loved ones in general. Actually, we do it quite frequently. However, when addiction is involved, the consequences may be more severe for all involved. Let me state clearly and loudly...You are not responsible for their behavior, nor have you done anything wrong. You have done the best you could with what you knew at the time. That is changing though, as reading this book makes evident.

Your loved one who suffers from addiction may have guilted you to come to their rescue or may have cursed you out for not doing so. Remember, addiction brings out manipulative schemes that you have been most susceptible to, because you love them and want to believe that they want to get better. This is fine, but I would suggest protecting yourself first, to enable you to be of maximum assistance. The addicted individual typically is problem saturated. You could inevitably consume yourself and the majority of your day with handling their responsibilities and fixing their issues and picking up the pieces of their broken life while they continue to abuse their drug of choice.

This will leave you exhausted, negatively affect your healthier relationships, and potentially bankrupt you financially or exacerbate your own medical conditions. I want you to imagine that you are standing in a Hula-Hoop. Go ahead and take a moment to visualize this. Literally, what can you directly control outside of your imaginary Hula-Hoop? Nothing, absolutely nothing.

Now we can begin with asserting healthy boundaries. If your loved one only calls or shows up when they need something, well, you have your first sign that there may be dysfunction in this relationship. Healthy relationships are reciprocal in nature. What about yours?

Boundaries and codependency are often discussed together. Even healthy relationships have codependent components and is referred to as interdependence when healthy and reciprocal for each others' mutual benefit. However, if your cycle resembles the Karpman Triangle, where you cycle through the roles of being the Accuser, to the Rescuer, and finish as the Victim-Repeat; then you may be in an unhealthy codependent relationship.

Please note that any attempts to break out of this cycle may elicit an uptick of aggression from your loved one. They have molded you to supply all of their needs and have refused to take accountability and responsibility for their own life. As you begin to shift their dependence and reliance from you being their main supporter, they are apt to become frustrated and disgruntled. Please use caution and protect yourself, physically and emotionally, from their backlash. You may need the support of others during this pivotal transition.

Most folks choose not to take the necessary steps to recover if their needs are still being met, even in sub-par conditions. They will drain or bleed every last ounce of support from you, and not have the wherewithal that they are doing such, nor have the necessary capacity to care. This is their addiction, not their essential self, which will be important to remember to spur the healing process for you and the relationship with them as they embrace recovery. It is important that you recognize the vicious nature of this process and the irrationality of the premise that you have been employing. Essentially, the more you do for them, the less they have to be responsible for. This strategic ploy has not been successful, so may I suggest ending it as soon as possible.

Once you recognize that these dynamics are unhealthy and not helpful to assist your loved one, you can become more grounded in your attempt to be of assistance. We have discussed that your loved one may react harshly to being cut off or from you taking a firmer approach with your allotted assistance and helping in their life.

This is to be expected and you should recognize that they may attempt to belittle you and tell you that you do not really love them, otherwise you would continue to help. Be prepared to answer this inquiry with a firm resolution. You may say something like this in your reply to them: "I refuse to be a part of your death" or "I simply will not participate in your self-destruction." This may sound similar to tough love, but remember, we are discussing how you can preserve your own well-being.

Chapter 21

Attempting to Save Your Current Relationship(s) and Other Considerations when Helping an Addicted Loved One

If you have been attempting to help a loved one who struggles with addiction, please take a moment to reflect on how this has affected your other relationships. Take a few minutes and simply consider how your time, financial, and emotional investments in your attempts to assist them has impacted others that you care about. Take another minute to reflect on the impact that this may have had on other family members or friends and how you would ideally like this to change in the future, starting now.

This may be challenging at first, because you have been on a life-saving mission, and it is easy to discard and minimize the impact that your efforts to help your loved one has had on others that you truly love and care about. If you have been fortunate to have a significant other or loved one or even a close friend to share your burden and tears with at times, well, I am truly happy for you because this is a wonderful source of support to sustain your continued efforts.

I asked that you take a moment to reflect on how your attempts to help the loved one who struggles with addiction has affected your other loved ones, as it most certainly has. I am not saying that it has had a devastating effect, but when you have diverted your time and attention to your loved one who struggles with addiction, it has taken away time and attention from your other relationships. I wanted to take a moment to address this and offer some tips on how you can still help your loved one, without fracturing other significant relationships in your life, especially if they are healthy and sustaining sources of love, care, and support.

First, simply acknowledging this fact to those important in your life can be tremendously healing. Those close to you who have been affected by your efforts to help your loved one may be understanding and not appear mad or upset. Yet, they may have desired some of your time and attention and have been upset when your loved one's antics have kept them from sharing more quality time with you.

Your love and desire for your loved one who is struggling has possibly created obsessional thoughts and feelings which has kept you from being emotionally present, even while you were with others that you genuinely care about. Over any considerable length of time, this can have an impact on the quality of any relationship(s) in your life, including your career.

You may have felt that others were pulling away from you or stopped asking how you were doing. They may have become upset with you when they heard some of the recent stories you have shared about your loved one and your attempts to help. They may have felt "less than" because your focus is on the loved one who is struggling while they have felt ignored, even though they have not done anything to deserve being given a lesser priority in your life. This is how family systems work, as each member affects the other members, even in indirect and hard to detect ways at times.

As you began to consider and realize the truth in this statement, it may open up future doors where you can take an active role to protect and nourish your meaningful relationships, while still being of assistance to your loved one who is struggling. Letting them know that you have recognized this fact and are willing to alter some of your current strategies is a wonderful step toward healing reconciliation.

Consider the following if you are married or have a significant other, regardless of whether they are the biological parent or not, of the loved one who is addicted. It is likely that your attempts to assist your loved one has probably created some discord, arguments, or other general disagreements over the years. Late-night phone calls, rearranging of plans and vacations, and other financial expenditures to bail them out (instead of accruing interest in a retirement account), have most likely created upset and unsettling feelings at the very least. Being open and honest about this will help you grasp a more secure foundation in your future attempts to help and be of assistance.

Attempting to get on the same page with your significant other or close family member about how you BOTH wish to proceed in your future attempts to assist is key. Creating the list of what you are willing and not willing to accept can help. Being transparent in your attempts to assist will also prove beneficial.

If there is still lingering anger from anyone close to you over past actions, asking them for forgiveness and being willing to make the appropriate amends is the next step. Letting them know that you are reading this book and have taken other steps to address your loved one's addiction can allow them to let down their guard, as they have potentially been hurt by your past actions and the veil of anger simply acts as a shield to their emotional vulnerability.

They most likely will intellectually understand the rationale and reasons why you have taken past actions in your attempt to help your loved one, but this does not mean that it will lessen the emotional impact that it has had on them. Investing in your current relationships will be vital in re-establishing healthy boundaries and supporting others you care about.

Examining your reasons for possibly unknowingly taking away from other relationships in your life to assist the one you love will be critical. This is simply another way that addiction impacts and robs the family system. Even though I would readily admit that most of this has been completely unintentional on your part, it is still worthwhile to address and actively take preventative steps to reduce future harm to these other significant relationships.

The others in your life who love and care about you deserve a similar devotion of your time and attention. My goal for highlighting this issue is to help to protect and honor these other relationships in a manner that you would desire, given your identified compassionate and caring qualities which motivated you to purchase this book.

I appreciate the opportunity to be of assistance to you and your family and truly do not want you to feel unnecessary guilt or upset for any unintentional effects that your past behaviors have had on others you truly care about. Remember, you have been doing the best you can with what you knew at the time. That is true for all of us. But now, properly armed with additional facts and resources, you can alter and adopt new thoughts and behaviors, which can be transformative to your life and relationships. That is the goal of this book, but brutal honesty is the key to psychological health and relational well-being.

Moving forward, take a moment to pause, and then consider how your attempts to help your loved one who struggles with addiction will impact others in your life. Adjust your behaviors accordingly. That is the relational dance you are currently in. Given that you do not have control over the behavior of others, simply focus on yourself, and your thoughts and behavior, which is all you or anyone has overt control over.

Make a statement or dedication to yourself and others you care about that you will not allow your loved one who is still struggling with addiction, to directly or indirectly, impact other important relationships in your life any longer. It is a choice you can make. Preserving your other significant relationships and cherishing them with love and with your presence will pay dividends emotionally for yourself and them.

Chapter 22
Dispelling Anger...
Cultivating Love

I would assume you struggle with or have struggled with feelings of anger that have distorted your view of your loved one at times based upon their actions. Anger is a God-given emotion. It can be channeled into helpful or motivating energy to continue your efforts in assisting them, if utilized appropriately. So, it may be helpful to explore the root causes of anger for your therapeutic benefit.

Anger is a secondary emotion. It can be helpful and healing to identify the primary emotion. To understand this, we need to examine how anger surfaces. Something happens or someone does something. You feel a primary emotion such as: hurt; fear; guilt; shame; embarrassment; humiliation; disrespect; frustration; irritation; jealousy; or resentment. Then, you choose to get Angry. I say choose because it is a choice. Anger feels more powerful than the primary emotion and offers you an illusion of control over the situation. However, anger is not helpful, and potentially hurtful to you and other relationships.

Therefore, eliminating anger from the equation can offer more fruitful results. Technically, we will discuss how you can manage anger better in the face of challenging circumstances, to offer yourself greater emotional balance and more grounded responses to the various antics and situations you find yourself involved in with your loved one.

The key is recognizing when you are angry, pausing, and having the awareness to identify what primary emotions are involved. Feeling hurt and experiencing fear can be overwhelming. These feelings can lead to emotional reactions and anger outbursts, but this will not change the dynamics nor assist the situation with your loved one in a helpful manner. Even though your ability to gain clarity and greater insight may not change the behavior of your loved one, you will reap the benefits of being more emotionally stable and experiencing less physical or medical symptoms as a result of your anger. That has been our focus throughout this book, to keep you well, in addition to offering helpful insights and suggestions to best assist your loved one who is addicted.

If you should find yourself angry or upset, pausing is key. Sit with it and ask yourself what other primary emotions may be underlying your anger. You will find one of the aforementioned emotions involved and then you have an opportunity to allow this emotion to take the forefront and calm your anger. You will also have the opportunity to experience greater congruence, as you are hurt by your loved one's actions and fearful for their life and well-being. This is completely natural and highlights our pursuit of displaying love in the face of difficult circumstances that you may find yourself in with your loved one.

Cultivating love, versus allowing yourself to be angry toward your loved one, will enhance your ability to influence their behavior and preserve your psychological well-being. I suggest that if you can dwell in love and come from a place of love, instead of allowing anger to resonate, you will feel more assured by some of the difficult decisions and actions that I have suggested throughout this book. Despite the outcome or success of your attempts to assist, you will be able to remain at peace with your decisions and avoid second-guessing your efforts, as you will have known that you came from a place of love and genuine concern. This may be a vital and necessary component to your overall well-being, especially if your attempts to assist do not produce the desired outcome, or even if less than desirable outcomes should transpire as part of your attempts to assist.

Think of your loved one, their essential being, remember their innocence, focus on the light in their soul, despite the dark cloud that has been hanging over them. Allow yourself to get in touch with this image prior to taking action or responding to any of their antics. You will find that you can be more resolute in your decision making and less apt to be coerced by their manipulative ploys to fulfill their self-centered needs and wishes. You will also find greater peace amid the distress and storms of life that they have created and may continue to stir up.

Love heals all wounds. It is love that dispels fear. We know that evil exists in the absence of love. We want to preserve and bring to the forefront your sincere and genuine love for your loved one, before proceeding in any communications with them or enacting your Action Plan when you feel you are ready to do so.

Chapter 23
Motivational Interviewing and ASAMs

This may be a little technical and academic in nature, but I thought it may be helpful or provide some insight to assist you in assessing or evaluating the severity of your loved one's addiction. ASAMs refer to the American Society of Addiction Medicine and the protocol that many addiction professionals and physicians utilize to guide the treatment of individuals who suffer from substance use disorders. It assesses the severity of the addiction issues and obstacles that may prevent a successful recovery on six dimensions.

Dimension 1 assesses the patient's Acute Intoxication and/or Withdrawal Potential. Obviously, if your loved one is impaired or high, efforts to assist will fall on deaf ears. Equally, if they are experiencing withdrawal, their sole focus from their "hijacked" brain is to obtain their drug of preference to stave off the pain of their withdrawal.

Dimension 2 assesses their Biomedical Condition and associated complications. Should they have a chronic medical condition or are simply generally in poor health due to their drug use, their ability to function or engage in treatment could be compromised. Hepatitis C and liver issues, along with other conditions, may affect cognitive functioning and should be addressed at the outset, as their efforts could stall because of underlying medical conditions.

Dimension 3 assesses their emotional, behavioral, or cognitive conditions and complications. It is helpful to explore their thoughts, emotions, and other mental health issues as this could play a factor in their treatment. Various substances can affect these issues in peculiar ways and can present an obstacle in assisting your loved one to engage in treatment.

Dimension 4 assesses their readiness to change. This is where certified Addiction Counselors and Licensed Practitioners earn their money. Most have been trained and utilize Motivational Interviewing when attempting to assist your loved one to engage in treatment. Motivational Interviewing is a non-confrontational approach designed to assist an individual through the various stages of change, allowing them to maintain their personal autonomy, which can be vital as part of this process.

Dimension 5 assesses their Relapse Potential, Continued Use, or Continued Problem Potential. This is vital in assisting the individual in the correct level of care. Some may benefit from Medication-Assisted Therapies, along with once a week counseling or community support group attendance. Others may need inpatient care.

Dimension 6 assesses their Recovery/Living Environment. It is hard to stay sober and avoid triggering people, places, and things. Assisting your loved one with safe housing or separating them from negative influences is key to their success, especially in the early stages of recovery.

Clinicians and Physicians utilize these dimensions to assist in placing your loved one in the appropriate level of care. I simply wished to demystify this process for you, and also assist you in gauging the severity of your loved one's problem. Every individual and situation are unique, but most practitioners would be able to assess your loved one via these dimensions to assist in guiding your loved one to the appropriate treatment program or most beneficial level of care.

Motivational Interviewing (MI) is a style of dialogue that many clinicians and others utilize to ask open-ended questions to assist a client to progress through the stages of change (a.k.a Transtheoretical Model of Behavior Change) which I will discuss later in this chapter. Clinicians utilizing MI express empathy through reflective listening. They develop discrepancy between clients' goals or values and their current behavior. They avoid arguments and direct confrontation. They adjust to client resistance rather than opposing it directly. They also support self-efficacy and optimism to bolster progress. These principles have been demonstrated to assist clients' progress through the following stages of change.

Stage One or Precontemplation is evident when the client is not thinking seriously about changing and is not interested in any kind of help. Clients in this stage tend to defend their maladaptive habits and do not recognize how problematic it is.

Stage Two or Contemplation can be observed when clients express being more aware of their maladaptive behaviors and are spending some time thinking about their issues, problems, and drug use as hindering them from their stated goals or life plans. They tend to be able to think about the possibility of change, though display ambivalence about doing so.

Stage Three or Preparation/Determination is where you see clients' make a commitment to change that can be evidenced by their statements or actions to seek appropriate information or resources to assist in facilitating this change.

They tend to be more desirous of improving the conditions in their life and are open to exploring options more so than the previous stages.

Stage Four or the Action stage is where clients believe that they possess the ability to change and have begun to take the actions to promote the changes they seek. They are actively involved in harm-reduction or abstinence-based recovery programs and are showing greater signs of healthy self-esteem and higher degrees of self-confidence.

Stage Five is the Maintenance/or Relapse component which involves the client being able to resist urges or temptations and maintain their sobriety or recovery, which in turns increases their self-efficacy. Of course, Relapse could occur at this stage and hopefully the successful utilization of resources up until this stage will allow the client to get back on the path of recovery quickly.

I wanted to share this with you for several reasons. One is to assist you in assessing where you feel your loved one is at currently. This could assist your efforts of being of assistance and minimize the frustrations experienced in doing so. If your loved one is in Precontemplation and does not recognize that their drug using behavior is problematic, the likelihood of them being open to intervention or changing their behavior is extremely low. By knowing this, you could assist with helping them recognize how their current choices could negatively impact their future health or trajectory in achieving success in life.

Addiction Professionals are trained in MI and utilize these principles to assist your loved one. They can help open their eyes to how their current behavior may keep them from achieving their stated goals or are counter to their values. They are trained to be able to listen carefully and adjust their interventions to be on par with your loved one's current stage, to assist them in keeping their autonomy and choose to progress to the next stage ideally.

ASAMs and MI assist clinicians in guiding your loved one to the appropriate level of care (Individual Therapy, IOP, or an Inpatient Stay) and can enhance the effectiveness of their treatment interventions. I also wanted to explore this process to allow you to take a more objective view of where your loved one may currently be in their thought and behavior processes to assist you in being more successful in your preparations to assist and intervene.

Chapter 24

What You May Say to Family and Children if Your Loved One Needs to Enter a Treatment Facility.

It is important to maintain a certain level of sensitivity and privacy when it comes to how to inform other individuals, including close relatives and children, when your loved one is to enter a treatment program or residential facility. There is still an abundance of negative stigmas associated with addiction and substance abuse, and this precludes individuals from entering treatment at times. I encourage you to limit your sharing on a need to know basis. Of course, you will need support through this time, and I am not discouraging you from reaching out to your support network. Yet, I would not recommend posting this occasion on your various social media platforms for all to know.

It is a great first step and your loved one has had to display a tremendous amount of courage and a humbling of their pride to accept treatment. I would like to discuss some of the pitfalls that can arise, and I hope this will assist in fostering the healthiest environment possible during and post-treatment.

Many individuals who enter treatment are concerned about what others will think. This includes their immediate family, parents, children, employers, friends, significant others, and possible Probation or Parole officers. Therefore, having a certain recited mantra could be of assistance to you, and them, and if handled successfully, could benefit all involved.

If your loved one has children, extra caution and sensitivity are highly recommended when discussing this issue. A rule of thumb you can use when speaking to young children is to consider how what you are about to share will affect their psychological and emotional well-being. If you cannot unequivocally cite how what you were getting ready to share would benefit them at the moment, then it may be best to limit details. What I mean by this, is that young children do not have the life experience or necessary understanding to process that their parent is in rehab for putting needles in their arm or drinking too much alcohol and blacking out.

A simpler version of this would be to say that Mommy or Daddy has a medical issue that they need to attend to, and they are getting specialized treatment to assist with their medical issue. Children are bright and have most likely recognized variations in the addicted parent's behavior and mood. Children will simply be delighted that their parent is getting the help they need on most occasions. Extra attention and a focus on keeping them emotionally well and occupied during this time can be of assistance. I have witnessed many families bring in grandparents or siblings to assist with this, as there will most likely be added stressors placed upon the primary caregiver of the home.

Consider yourself (and them) fortunate if this is an option.

It is also important to make sure the children can express their feelings. It may be helpful to speak with them about how they feel about their parent being gone. Reassure and validate them, as necessary. I would also encourage you to seek out professional counseling services for the children, as Licensed Therapists can be of great assistance during this time. Many therapists incorporate Play Therapy in their practice, which can be extremely helpful to young children with a limited feeling vocabulary to express or demonstrate how they are feeling. Therapy can help children get the additional appropriate support to sustain them during this time.

I have already discussed that your loved one will be especially sensitive upon being discharged, or throughout the treatment process. Please remember that they have been using chemicals to mood alter, and if they are now sober, they are likely to react as a raw nerve in times of increased stress or strife. Hopefully, their initial treatment process will provide them with some healthy coping mechanisms that will assist in ameliorating some of these negative emotions, but you can also be of some assistance to them in this process.

Utilizing a need to know basis is helpful, but I am sure close relatives and friends will have questions. I cannot be certain of what you may need to share with these individuals, but simply stating they have struggled with a substance use disorder and they are getting the help they need, is a plain and simple start. Requesting that other loved ones respect their privacy can also be helpful. When your loved one is released from treatment, they may become impatient with frequent questions about how they are doing. They may also become upset with you for sharing where they have been and what they were doing.

I simply encourage you to use discretion and think about what will best assist them in their efforts to recover. You are not responsible for their behavior or reactions, but they will also appear emotionally immature in their reactions, and my hope is to temper or avoid some of these unnecessary pitfalls.

When speaking to their employer, if necessary, simply let them know they went to an in-patient treatment program or need to request a leave of absence. You may be best served by working with the Human Resources department (if applicable) regarding these issues. They may be eligible for FMLA (Family and Medical Leave Act) or short-term disability benefits. Of course, this will be a case by case situation.

It would be best if you allow your loved one who is going to treatment or is in treatment to deal directly with their employer or other entities, including Probation or Parole Departments. This will be a healthy first step to correct dysfunctional codependency patterns that may have evolved and protect you from being blamed for any negative outcomes. They are responsible for their lives and behavior, not you.

Chapter 25

Your Action Plan to Help Your Loved One Who is Suffering from Addiction

Throughout this book, I have purposefully shifted the focus on what you can do to assist and keep yourself well, and sane, as you attempt to help your loved one. This is and will be of vital importance as you proceed. I sincerely hope that some of the information and suggestions have been helpful thus far. I have tried my best to provide you with accurate and truthful information from various perspectives, to present a well-rounded methodology on how you can be of maximum benefit to your loved one who is addicted.

If you have made it this far, I hope this chapter will assist in you feeling comfortable taking action to promote greater health and wellness for all parties involved. I would encourage you to first start by rallying support from anyone in your life who is willing to go along on this journey with you. This will be vitally important as we navigate the upcoming days, weeks, and months of early recovery for your loved one.

I would assume that you have jotted down some ideas or had some thoughts about what the most practical approach to assisting your loved one may be as you have been reading and reviewing this book. This would be a good place to start in the formulation of your action plan. Please recognize that you and your loved one may have to adjust some of this action plan as it begins to unfold, as you incorporate ever-changing conditions that moving toward sobriety and sustained recovery can present.

First, review your ultimate goal for your loved one. Hopefully, this will become their ultimate goal too. Sobriety and sustained recovery, in whatever form this may take, would be ideal.

Now we can begin to break this goal down into achievable components. If your loved one is still actively using or drinking, our first goal should be to separate them, via safe and medically appropriate means as necessary, from their drug of choice. They need to stop using alcohol and/or drugs before we can begin to assist with helping them build their foundation that can support their recovery.

This is where some of your hardest decisions and choices will most likely need to be made. Having the support of family, friends, or other professionals will be vital during this earliest, and likely erratic stage. Having a template of a plan is also vital for you, as your loved one will most likely challenge every step, kicking and screaming (at least emotionally or physiologically) during this early stage.

You will need to aptly define what you are not willing to accept any longer. This will take the shape and form that you will feel most uncomfortable with at first, but I would encourage you to trust your gut, intuition, or inner voice as to what is best. You will have to give yourself prior approval and acceptance of any negative communications or reactions from your loved one during this stage.

Remember that their brain is hijacked, and that drug-seeking is now their primary instinctual drive and is motivating their less than ideal reactive behavior. Please do not proceed with this action plan formally, until you feel that you have the steadfast determination to persevere in your efforts, knowing you are truly attempting to save their life.

Once you feel that you have achieved the necessary fortitude to proceed, ideally with support, communicate with your loved one on how you would like to assist and offer help as you are able. Let them know that you only want the best for them and that you have taken time to find resources that could be of assistance, in the form of doctors, counselors, or treatment facilities, that may offer them another way of life.

Please attempt to keep all communications civil, whether in person or via text or phone calls. Do not take the bait if they react with vehement anger and make audacious comments about you personally. This is their addicted brain responding, and their addiction simply wants the drug intake to continue. Hopefully, by the time you are enacting this plan, you have already chosen to alter your communication style with your loved one to ease this process. If not, well, now is the time to do so.

I want you to write out concisely what you are willing to do, and what you are no longer willing to accept. Keep a copy of this and give a copy of this to your loved one. Sticking to it will be the hardest part, understandably.

I strongly encourage some sort of medical intervention in the beginning stages. Years or decades of drug abuse can take a toll on the body. There may be other physical conditions that may need to be tended to in these early stages. Of course, if inpatient treatment is an option, many of these facilities will have a medical provider or staff to assist with this.

If your loved one is not planning to go to inpatient for any variety of reasons, identifying competent medical providers to include physicians or programs that prescribe Suboxone®, Methadone, Vivitrol®, or Antabuse (depending on their drug of preference) would be the logical next step if you or they feel they would benefit from medications to stabilize in early recovery. Also, identifying out-patient treatment programs or Licensed Therapists who specialize in addiction treatment will be helpful.

Make your loved one aware of community support groups such as Alcoholics Anonymous, Narcotics Anonymous, and Celebrate Recovery. There are numerous support groups such as Sex & Love Addicts Anonymous, Overeaters Anonymous, Cocaine Anonymous, and countless others for almost any maligned subject of human behavior. I will place a list of various recovery resources on my own website to assist.

Hopefully, your loved one will accept your offer and choose to receive help. This may occur and you can assist and support them in their recovery efforts as you wish, as long as you feel it is a healthy decision for you to do so.

However, should your loved one not be open to accepting help, then I encourage you to enact your plan based upon what you had already pre-determined that you were no longer willing to tolerate or accept in regards to your loved one's behavior. If they simply choose to refuse help and keep using, well, now you have a choice to make.

You could try again to intervene or offer help at a later time, or you could take immediate steps to protect yourself and your other family members. I would assume that you have a notion of what the next right decision should be based upon the other information in this book and your experience with your loved one.

It may require courage and a certain boldness to break their pattern of addiction by removing yourself from the equation. To assist in bolstering your efforts should this be your decision, let me remind you that this may also be the necessary shake-up to the Family System that jars your loved one to a momentary clarity that will open their eyes to their twisted and sordid reality.

Chapter 26

Slaying your own Dragons and Finding Support

Please do not be offended by my insinuation that you may benefit from taking a look at your own lifestyle to identify areas that may need or deserve attention and healing. In my personal and professional experience, and as research makes clear, addiction is a family disease. A loved one's addiction impacts the entire family. You have witnessed this. So, I am simply encouraging you to take an honest look at your life and relationships and visualize how you would ideally like it to be more holistically healthy.

Whether this means that you began exercising or eating healthier, attending church or other spiritual activities, or take up a new hobby or start a new home improvement project, I would encourage you to look for ways to expand your wellness. Of course, if there are glaring issues that impede your ability to appropriately assist your loved one, then I would encourage you to locate the resources that can assist you in striving for greater overall health.

I had to say that so I could say the following; if you have struggled with alcohol or other drugs (formerly or currently), please take time to assist yourself as part of this journey. Hopefully, some of the information contained thus far will be helpful. If you no longer struggle with such vices but did in the past, it may be wise to seek outside help in the form of counseling to identify any lingering guilt or shame from your past behaviors that you feel may have contributed to your loved one's current issues. These lingering negative emotions could be blocking or impeding your objectivity. Being able to take a depersonalized perspective will benefit you in assisting your loved one through the difficult days and months ahead. Not doing so may prevent you from being of optimal support, which is what you have been desiring to be, understandably.

I do not wish to sound presumptuous, but if there was a family history of addiction or alcoholism in the prior generations, well, these old unhealthy dynamics of the family system could have been subliminally passed down through you (if you are the parent, or from your partner's epigenetic lineage) unknowingly. As you proceed, you will benefit from having the clearest vision possible regarding examining and acting accordingly in your relationships. Being able to have a healthy and objective perspective and a keen awareness on the conditions in the family that preceded you and contributed to your current family dynamics may be a priceless source of knowledge, as the days and months ahead may be messy emotionally, at best.

Being able to be honest with yourself and others is a vital trait to sustain your loved one's recovery. This is also an important step for you to take as part of this process. The more honest you are with yourself, the less defensive you will be if and when your loved one redirects the attention to possible errors of your own in the past. We are not perfect people, and most of us would make healthier decisions with the wisdom we carry today, as opposed to what was available to us some time ago.

My encouragement for you to take a look at your own life and behaviors (past and present) is simply meant to be holistically reaffirming for you and place you on a solid foundation of wellness for your life to enable you to appropriately assist your loved one. I will not attempt to imagine the pain, sacrifices, or horror that you may have had to witness from your own childhood and from watching your loved one slowly dissipate regarding health and wellness. These may have been some of the most traumatizing things you have ever had to endure. My goal for you is that you will take responsibility for own your life in much the same manner that you wish that your loved one will do for theirs.

Please take some time to reflect on how you can promote your overall wellness and make an action plan that you can begin to implement immediately, not tomorrow. "I'll quit tomorrow" may have already been echoed by your loved one. You can be a shining example to them starting now.

Chapter 27

Reasons to Continue Despite Past Unsuccessful Efforts

I find it safe to assume that if you are reading this book, it is because you have already attempted to assist your loved one, but these attempts have not been successful. It would be understandable that you and others may question as to why you choose to continue to want to help them when they appear to not want to help themselves. From a casual observer perspective, this is a relevant question.

I also understand that you love them and would most likely give up your own life for theirs (if you are the parent in many cases), and that giving up is not an option that you can live with. I applaud your efforts, regardless of the apparent lack of long-term success up to this point. I encourage you to keep attempting to be of assistance to them and hope that some of the information contained in this book will boost your efforts (and success rates).

Your loved one who struggles with an addiction deserves your time and energy. By this point in their addiction, they have probably lost several meaningful relationships and burnt numerous bridges because of their addiction. They most likely do not have many folks left in their corner that are willing to support and encourage them, understandably.

I hope you are able to revitalize your efforts and determination with some of the information contained in this book. I hope you will reach out to others to add the necessary and sustained support that will be needed as you continue in your efforts to be of assistance. Never giving up is a sure-fire method for continuing to make progress. I, nor you, will ever know when the seed we may have planted some time ago takes root. We can move forward with good cheer, praying and asking for this day to be soon, in God's time and wisdom. God is in control, and we can simply follow His will for our lives and ask that He be with our loved one and protect and guide them. We can do the legwork, however, given our close proximity to them here on Earth.

I have attempted to emphasize that you must come from a place of love and understanding to be most effective. Having examined and re-mediated your own issues to be able to present a calm and centered emotional approach will be vital. Your loved one most likely recognizes (to the depth of their capability at their current usage or impaired state) the pain and suffering they have caused you. Unless they are steeped in antisocial behaviors and attitudes (which is quite possible by the late stages of addiction), they will feel guilt and shame for what their life-style choices have led to and the impact it has had on your life

Recognizing a sincere attempt on your part to simply assist them in alleviating further suffering for all parties involved will possibly net you the most successful results. I have offered numerous strategies to assist you in your efforts to view the current situation practically and objectively for what it is. I hope that you will take these suggestions and implement them for your well-being and the subsequent well-being of your loved one who suffers from addiction issues. I have purposefully utilized an action-oriented tone to prompt you to take the life-saving actions that could benefit you and them.

Conclusion

I hope this book has better prepared you to be there for your loved one who suffers from addiction. I have attempted to highlight aspects of the addiction process and typical dynamics that occur in most loved one's attempts to intervene. It is my intent to be helpful, and I appreciate your willingness to trust some of my tips and suggestions. I pray that the information in this book will be helpful in your pursuit to assist your loved one.

Addiction is completely irrational to the observer. It simply does not make sense and will drive you batty trying to understand it or your loved one's behavior at times. Yet, the power of love and dedication can be a tremendous force to combat the irrationality. Keep yourself well, talk to others who can understand, and above all, maintain HOPE.

The power of hope has been discussed by many experts, theologians, and philosophers. It can sustain your efforts even through the dim or dark tunnels that your loved one's addiction may take you through. I truly hope that some of my words will resonate with you and provide a pathway or give you an insight into how you could more effectively be of assistance to your loved one.

I know that you may not always be successful in your attempts. Please remember that you can only plant the seeds of recovery, and it is up to your loved one to nourish these seeds into maturation. Keep planting the seeds.

The fact that you keep trying to assist lets them know (at least on a subconscious level) that you love them and are there for them if they desire help. This fact should not be taken for granted. Their addiction will ruin many of their vital relationships, but the ones that are connected by the heartstrings of a loved one may just be the vital missing link in helping them realize their purpose and meaning in this world when all else is lost. Don't take this away from them.

You should be congratulated on your courageous spirit to go to the ends of the earth to help pull them out of the pits of their addiction hell. Stories of recovery abound on the internet and in books, by those who have successfully regained their lives and souls from addiction. Allow yourself to live vicariously at times through their stories of recovery to keep your spirits up when things look bleak.

Life has meaning, and their life has meaning. Help them see this. Love them. Pray for them. Keep yourself well. My thoughts and prayers will be with you. Feel free to reach out to me via email to let me know how things are going if you would like. I will respond as I am able.

Personal Reflection

I am a person who has been fortunate to be in long-term recovery. My life has fundamentally changed, positively, and has been revolutionized in ways that were once unimaginable. I wanted to take a moment to provide you an in-depth understanding and perspective from someone who has struggled with addiction and alcoholism.

I grew up in a resort town where social cues and influences were set to "party" (used as a verb). From a relatively young age in my early and mid-teenage years, I found it necessary and fun to enjoy alcohol and other drugs for recreational purposes. I experienced blackouts and car accidents as a result of my impairment numerous times. This continued into my college years. Eventually, I had become a maintenance drinker, which required me to have a certain amount of alcohol in my bloodstream to avoid having grand mal seizures. This is when I crossed the line from wanting to drink and use drugs, to having to drink and use drugs.

The hospital visits started occurring more frequently, and I was even in a coma for several days with two regions in my brain hemorrhaging simply from my alcohol and drug use. One would think that this would be enough to open one's eyes to the potential dangers of their use and force them to quit. Not me, I was determined.

Actually, after regaining consciousness from being in a coma, and upon being placed in my own hospital room with a morphine drip attached intravenously, I asked one of my friends to bring in several mini-bottles of vodka, given the hospital provided me with OJ and Cranberry juice in my room. I tell you this not to highlight my escapades; rather, to illustrate the depth of depravity I was enduring regarding my alcoholism. I checked myself out of the hospital later that day against medical advice because I wanted to smoke a cigarette.

I would love to tell you that my story of recovery began there, but I had to suffer several more years of dragging along my bottom before my moment of clarity transpired. This included being jobless, homeless, friendless, and faithless. I remember the looks and faces of those passing by, which exuded a mixture of pity and disgust as I aimlessly roamed the streets of Downtown Charleston, South Carolina during this low point of my life and addiction.

Then, one day, my brother who had witnessed my decline firsthand at times, simply asked me the following: "Bruce, don't you ever get tired of drinking?" In his carefully crafted question delivered with a non-judgmental tone... a monumental shift in my perspective on life occurred... seriously. I was tired of drinking, as it had been years since it had been fun. I said "Yes", and he asked if I was okay with his wife searching for options for me to get help.

As soon as I became willing, doors began to miraculously open. As mentioned, I knew I needed medical detoxification as I would have a seizure if I was separated from alcohol for a prolonged period (12-24 hours roughly I assume). I made a phone call during this time period to a friend who I used to "party" with. Her mother answered and informed me that she had recently entered a treatment program. I told her mother that I was thinking about going to treatment as well and another door opened.

I checked into a medical detoxification facility on February 5th, 2003. I consider February 6th, 2003, the first day of my sobriety and have celebrated, by the "Grace of God Alone," continuous sobriety & recovery since that date. Thank You, Jesus! My journey in recovery has had its share of life issues. I have been fortunate to have good mentors. I listened to others who were once like me, or worse, and did what they suggested, which had helped them learn a new way to live and cope with life on life's terms without depending on chemicals. My life sober has been amazing, truly, and I would have sold myself short in my first months or years of recovery had I created a goal or list of objectives for my future other than being sober one day at a time. That is because they would not have been able to encompass or contain what is now my new, wonderful, and sober everyday reality. Again, I have gone through life issues, but I have not found it necessary to pick up a drink or drug, and things seem to always work out. New doors continue to open.

I am telling you this, not to boast, but simply to inspire hope that your loved one could find the same on their own path of recovery. Having witnessed thousands of stories of recovery by this point in my life and career, I know it is possible. I want you to be able to have a similar conviction as you set forth on being of maximum service to your loved one who is struggling with addiction.

I truly hope that some of the information contained in this book will assist you and your loved one on this journey called Life. The fact that you have reached out and picked up a book that could assist speaks volumes about your love and good intentions for your loved one and yourself. I know that every situation is unique, and that circumstances and resources vary widely. I have attempted to present a concise picture of how you can be of assistance to your loved one during this time, in a manner that could be accessible by nearly anyone regardless of resources. It is my hope that some of the information contained will either help you or them, or ideally both, surpass the challenges that addiction presents.

It is with humble appreciation and a deep sense of profound gratitude that I say thank you and wish you and your loved one wellness, peace, and prosperity.

Respectfully,

Bruce A. Lynch

Made in the USA
Columbia, SC
24 September 2021